D0149091

# Philo of Alexandria

# OTHER OXFORD BOOKS
## BY SAMUEL SANDMEL

We Jews and Jesus

The Enjoyment of Scripture

The Hebrew Scriptures

The First Christian Century in Judaism and Christianity

Ed., The New English Bible: Oxford Study Edition

Judaism and Christian Beginnings

# Philo of Alexandria

## AN INTRODUCTION

Samuel Sandmel

New York                      Oxford
OXFORD UNIVERSITY PRESS
1979

Copyright © 1979 by Samuel Sandmel

Library of Congress Cataloging in Publication Data

Sandmel, Samuel.
    Philo of Alexandria.

    Bibliography: p.
    Includes index.
    1.  Philo Judaeus.  I.  Title.
B689.Z7S28      181'.3      78–10630
ISBN  0–19–502514–8
ISBN  0–19–502515–6 pbk.

Printed in the United States of America

To Professor Valentin Nikiprowetzky
in gratitude for an unusually careful reading of my manuscript

# Preface

My cherished teacher, Erwin R. Goodenough, published his *An Introduction to Philo Judaeus* in 1940. In the lapse of almost forty years there has been an immense amount written that needs attention, and that is the most compelling reason for my undertaking the present work. I have taught a course in Philo annually for over twenty-five years; recurrently students have told me that they found Goodenough's book difficult, and several have told me how helpful his book was on re-reading it at the end of the course. I have tried to discover what in Goodenough's book appeared difficult, and I have made the effort here to write in a way easier for the beginner. This intention has made repetitions necessary or at least desirable. I hope that I am less repetitious than Philo himself.

Professor Goodenough had some very special theories about Philo, and I have devoted a chapter to the matter. Respecting some of the areas of the controversies about Philo, I have regarded it as my task here to subordinate my own partisan views, or else to label them clearly enough to be identifiable, for it is my wish to introduce a beginner to Philo, and to let him, after this introduction, proceed to fashion his own biases.

Some scholars have adulated Philo, some have scorned him. While I can live tranquilly with the scorn of Philo as a shabby thinker and with the view that he was profundity itself, I cannot live tranquilly with the neglect of him. The specialist in Jewish studies, especially the Tannaitic age of the Greco-Roman period, or the specialist in early Christianity is simply incomplete and deficient if he does not have some firsthand acquaintance with Philo. I do not mean an acquaintance with my book, and I surely do not mean an acquaintance through reading a brief excerpt or two in some anthology; I mean an acquaintance through reading entire treatises in which Philo "explains" the Bible. Whether Philo was truly great, or only an ordinary mind in a man who wrote a tremendous amount, the student of religious and philosophical movements in his age who ignores him does so at his own peril.

S.S.

*Cincinnati, Ohio*
*1978*

# Contents

# Abbreviations
# of Philo's Treatises

| | |
|---|---|
| *Abr.* | *De Abrahamo* |
| *Aet.* | *De Aeternitate Mundi* |
| *Agr.* | *De Agricultura* |
| *Cher.* | *De Cherubim* |
| *Conf.* | *De Confusione Linguarum* |
| *Congr.* | *De Congressu Quaerendae Eruditionis Gratia* |
| *Decal.* | *De Decalogo* |
| *Det.* | *Quod Deterius Potiori Insidiari Soleat* |
| *Deus* | *Quod Deus Sit Immutabilis* |
| *Ebr.* | *De Ebrietate* |
| *Flacc.* | *In Flaccum* |
| *Fug.* | *De Fuga et Inventione* |
| *Gig.* | *De Gigantibus* |
| *Her.* | *Quis Rerum Divinarum Heres Sit* |
| *Hyp.* | *Hypothetica* |
| *Jos.* | *De Josepho* |
| *L.A.* I, II, III | *Legum Allegoriae* |
| *Leg.* | *De Legatione ad Gaium* |

| | |
|---|---|
| *Mig.* | *De Migratione Abrahami* |
| *Mos.* I, II | *De Vita Mosis* |
| *Mut.* | *De Mutatione Nominum* |
| *Op.* | *De Opificio Mundi* |
| *Plant.* | *De Plantatione* |
| *Post.* | *De Posteritate Caini* |
| *Praem.* | *De Praemiis et Poenis* |
| *Prob.* | *Quod Omnis Probus Liber* |
| *Prov.* | *De Providentia* |
| *Sac.* | *De Sacrificiis Abelis et Caini* |
| *Sob.* | *De Sobrietate* |
| *Som.* I, II | *De Somniis* |
| *Spec.* I, II, III, IV | *De Specialibus Legibus* |
| *Virt.* | *De Virtute* |
| *Vita* | *De Vita Contemplativa* |

## Other Abbreviations

| | |
|---|---|
| Sandmel | *Philo's Place in Judaism* |
| Wolfson | *Philo* (2 vols.) |
| Goodenough | *Introduction to Philo Judaeus* |
| Goodenough, BLL | *By Light, Light: The Mystic Gospel of Hellenistic Judaism* |
| LCL | Loeb Classical Library |

# I

# I

## Introduction

Philo, usually alluded to as Philo Judaeus ("the Jew"), wrote of himself as an "old man,"[1] this around the year 42/43 A.D. Presumably he was born about 25 or 20 B.C.; the date of his death can be guessed at as around A.D. 50. His lifetime overlapped that of Herod the Great; the Rabbinic sages Hillel, Shammai, and Gamaliel (the latter mentioned in Acts of the Apostles); Jesus and Paul. He was a native of Alexandria in Egypt, and hence he reflects Jewish life and experience outside Judea.

These brief statements, presently to be amplified, are the clues to the externals that make Philo a figure of some importance. Since he died before the Romans destroyed the Temple in A.D. 70 and thereby ended the Temple cult, the Temple had living significance for him. But in his life as a Jew remote from that Temple, his writings reflect some ingredients of Synagogue Judaism, the Judaism that flourished in local centers and which survived after Temple Judaism ended.

Philo makes no mention of any Christian person or event.[2] Yet the New Testament was written in Greek in the Greco-Roman world, not in Hebrew or Aramaic in Judea, and hence in an environment in some sense similar to that in which Philo flourished. Aspects of the New Testament, such as the Epistles of Paul, the Gospel According to John, and the Epistle to the Hebrews, exhibit some affinity to ideas found in Philo—and we shall look at these.[3]

Moreover, Philo was a sort of a Platonist; the opinion, ascribed to Numenius,[4] was that "either Philo platonizes or Plato philonizes." He also was a kind of Stoic: these matters will be clarified later. Philo is useful, accordingly, for the understanding of the later Greek philosophy, such as Middle Stoicism, Neo-Pythagoreanism, Middle Platonism, and even Neo-Platonism.

As a legatee of both Jewish and Greek culture, Philo reflects so much of what he inherited that the question has been raised as to how much of the abundance he wrote is original, or else, how valuable it is. Modern scholars have expressed judgments on Philo that range from unlimited admiration to contempt itself. Harry Wolfson[5] ascribes to Philo a profundity, and an achievement, that would put Philo into the select circle of the few very great minds in the history of philosophy. Others have not shared Wolfson's extreme admiration.

The range of diverse judgments is a result partly of the uniqueness of Philo in representing the first major blend of Judaism and Hellenism, and partly because of the nature of his writings. These are for the most part expositions of Scripture; in this exposition he utilizes a method known as allegory, a method that, as we shall see, allowed him to interpret Scripture in terms of Platonism and Stoicism. If one grants that Platonism and Stoicism are present in virtually every paragraph that Philo wrote on Scripture, the question arises, is there some plus beyond these which would make Philo something other than merely an echoer of ideas already expressed? Against Wolfson's assertion that there is, Richard Reitzenstein asserts that there is not,[6] for he contended that to deem Philo an eclectic was unduly to honor him.

From a different standpoint, another question can be asked: Granted that the substance of Philo's biblical exposition is philosophical, was his purpose to set forth philosophy, or is the philosophy only incidental to a different purpose? If the philosohy is at best incidental, might it not be more appropriate to call Philo, as Emil Schuerer[7] does, essentially a psychologist? Such varying opinions about Philo emerge from the modern scrutiny of his philosophy-like writings, not from any ancient description or ancient assessment of the man.

Voluminous as his surviving writings are (requiring thirteen books in the Loeb Classical Library version), specific information about the man, to which we shall turn, is exceedingly scanty. This case of scant information applies also to the Jewish community of Alexandria as a whole. We know something about its great size and about its importance, but direct information about the community itself is surprisingly limited. We know that Jews appear to have settled in Alexandria right from its founding. After Alexander the Great (356–323 B.C.) had conquered Palestine in 332, he moved on to take Egypt away from the Persians. In 332/331 near the mouth of the Nile, he founded the city of Alexandria, destined to become a new commercial and cultural center for the eastern Mediterranean. An architect, Deinocrates, laid out the plans for the projected city on the mainland, protected by an island known as Pharos. A breakwater was built from the mainland to the island, getting its name, Heptastadia ("seven stadia"), from its length, a *stadion* measuring about 625 feet. The island and the breakwater made the harbor very well protected. After the death of Alexander, Egypt fell to his general, Ptolemy Lagos; the subsequent growth and development of Alexandria was accomplished under the Ptolemies.

In due course the carefully planned city was divided into three districts respecting its inhabitants; in Philo's time, five districts seem to have emerged. The western part of Alexandria was occupied chiefly by Egyptians. The northeast portion was occupied by Jews. The other part, destined to grow even larger, was

Greek and the center of royalty in the dynasty of the Ptolemies.

The commercial prosperity of Alexandria led to its becoming a cultural center of great significance. A so-called "Museum" was in reality a kind of university, including both a library and a theater. Within a century after its founding, Alexandria surpassed Carthage in size and eminence, and was apparently second only to Rome itself.

Under the Ptolemies, Alexandria was ruled locally by a Senate, as were two other Egyptian cities, Naucratis and Ptolemais. Precisely how much autonomy was allowed the cities is not certain. The term, "an Alexandrian," came to have a connotation different from the merely geographical; it implied what we would call the "rights of citizenship," rights that were by no means possessed by all its residents. When in 30 B.C. Egypt passed into the control of Rome (whose influence in Egypt was felt as early as 180 B.C.), it became a province, governed by a prefect directly responsible to the Roman Emperor. Yet Alexandria was grudgingly allowed to retain its local autonomy, and also its Senate, these stemming from Ptolemaic times.

The Roman historians stress that Egypt in general and Alexandria in particular were hotbeds of both resentment against Rome and rebelliousness. That Egypt was ruled by a prefect subject not to the Roman Senate but to the Emperor himself reflects the Roman anxiety about the stability of the Roman rule there. Culturally, Alexandria and its eminence challenged the supremacy of Rome. Politically, there existed some adversary presumptions between Alexandria and Rome. In the areas in which Rome was suspicious of Alexandria, the Jews of Alexandria were an additional factor of Roman disquietude. In other words, Rome had its problems with Alexandria. The Jews there constituted a complication to those problems.

The Jewish community in Philo's time was immense, outnumbering the Jewish population of Judea. Philo (*Flaccus* 43) speaks of the Jewish population of Egypt as more than a million. Modern demographers do not fully accept this figure but are agreed that the population was huge.[8] Philo speaks of the many synagogues that existed in Alexandria. Rabbinic tradition mentions a sort of "great synagogue" of great size and luxury, but this may be only legendary.[9]

Were the Jews of Alexandria "Alexandrians"? What was their political status before Egypt became Roman? What was it after? Answers to such important questions are elusive, for the sources provide neither full nor clear information.

What does seem right is that there was in Roman times a legacy from the previous Ptolemaic age of a very large measure of Jewish autonomy, such as had been granted to Jews in various areas of the eastern Mediterranean by Greek rulers. Such autonomy in general terms allowed Jews to live under, and to govern themselves by, Jewish laws, with the rulers ordinarily protecting this autonomy. The rights of the Jews usually included exemptions from obligations that would impede fidelity to Jewish laws. They included the privilege of observing without interference Jewish sacred days, whether the Sabbath or the festivals, and apparently provided some exemption of Jews from enrollment in the military, since such enrollment would impede the fidelity to Jewish laws.

At what point did such Jewish self-government imply a political status which granted fewer than the fullest rights of citizenship? Egyptians, as distinct from Greeks in Egypt, did not have full rights. But were the Alexandrian Jews "Alexandrians" in the fullest sense? In *Against Apion* II, 28 ff., Josephus attacks the "anti-Semite" Apion in the following terms: Apion was an Egyptian born in the "oasis" (the "Great Oasis" in Upper Egypt); he had moved to Alexandria, repudiated his Egyptian origin so as to be considered a Greek, and, receiving the rights of citizenship, falsely claimed to be an "Alexandrian." Josephus goes on to say that the Jews of Alexandria had settled in the northeast, on the seaboard, which was "by universal consent its finest residential quarter"; that part of the city had been presented to them by Alexander the Great, and, important to our context, they had been granted *isopoliteia*[10] ("parity in citizenship") with the Macedonians. Local Alexandrian Jews, says Josephus, still bore the name of Macedonians. The rights that had been bestowed on the Jews were recorded in the papers of the Ptolemies; they had been recorded on a stele by Julius Caesar, who had thereby publicly declared that the Jews were citizens of Alexandria.[11] Josephus, in ridiculing Apion for "his astonishment at the very idea of Jews being called Alexandrians," goes on to say that the Jews of Antioch were called Antiochenes, and so too elsewhere. Josephus then reviews the history of the rights granted the Jews of Alexandria by the succession of Ptolemies and the high military rank achieved by certain Jewish generals. The maltreatment of the Jews by Cleopatra (died 31 B.C.) was a fact of which the Jews could be proud. That is to say, Josephus not only attacks Apion but he asserts the political equality of the Alexandrian Jews.

But the documents which he provides elsewhere (especially in *Antiquities*, Book XIV) are not taken at face value by many modern scholars, especially by Victor Tcherikover.[12] That there is "forgery" in the documents, or that whole documents are forgeries, is a frequent though contested conclusion among scholars. If there was indeed forgery, it might have been present already in the documents Josephus quotes, or he himself may have been the forger. Tcherikover's conclusion respecting Jews of Alexandria is negative, that is, Jews did not possess fullest equality in the matter of civil rights, despite the term *isopoliteia* which Josephus used.

Tcherikover's view rests on a document, ordinarily called a "rescript," issued by the Emperor Claudius, to which we presently turn. This Rescript is to be kept quite separate from a "Letter" of Claudius. The Letter of Claudius appears in Josephus,

*Antiquities* XIX, 280–85; the Rescript is a papyrus discovered in the nineteenth century.[13]

The pertinent difference between the Letter and the Rescript is the following: the Letter of Claudius reproduced in Josephus implies the Jews have full rights of citizenship in Alexandria, while the Rescript imposes, or better, reimposes, the limitation of barring Jews from entrance into the *gymnasia*, the institutions for the pursuit of the so-called "encyclical" studies (in somewhat the same way that in parts of nineteenth-century Europe Jews were legally barred from the universities and in the twentieth were excluded from private social and country clubs). Moreover, the Rescript directly contradicts Josephus by denying that Jews are Alexandrians, terming them instead foreigners merely resident in Alexandria. The authenticity of the Letter has been challenged by modern scholars; the authenticity of the Rescript has gone unchallenged. Some time later than the Rescript, Claudius is said to have expelled Jews from Rome, and this datum is used to buttress the authenticity of the Rescript, since it shows some hostility to Jews.

Rights, but not fullest rights, would seem an appropriate way to characterize Diaspora Jewish citizenship. Generous but not unreserved rights enabled Jewish communities to develop their own inner institutions, such as synagogues, schools, law courts, and philanthropic activities. As to an important matter in regard to Jewish privileges, namely, the relation of Jews to pagan deities, Tcherikover makes a point of some consequence. While in practice Jews seem to have been exempted from the obligation to participate in the worship of the Greek gods, there is no specific mention of this exemption in any of the many documents that Josephus quotes. Tcherikover believes that the absence of specific mention of this exemption is not due to chance. Rather he asks if "anyone—whether Greek king, Roman governor, or Greek city —[could] write the words: 'I permit the Jews not to respect the

Gods.' "[14] His reasonable conclusion is that it was habitual rather than strictly legal for Jews to abstain from the worship of Greek gods, and from regarding the emperor as a god. Emperor worship had begun in the East, where Augustus Caesar received that great honor which was not given him in the city of Rome. Divine honors were passingly sought by the Emperor Tiberius and openly by his successor Gaius Caligula, in whose reign (37–41) there was a large-scale uprising against the Jews of Alexandria. Gaius also gave orders to place an image of himself in the Temple in Jerusalem, but heeded his representatives who had first abstained from carrying out the order and then persuaded him to withdraw it. Except in the case of Gaius Caligula, Jews seem to have had no difficulties in abstaining from emperor worship.

We have said that we inherit very little information about the inner workings of the Alexandrian Jewish community. The writings of Philo are in a sense notable in that they are largely marked both by this lack, as well as other lacks. Stray clues here and there suggest a council of elders numbering seventy-one, and also an "ethnarch," that is, a ruler responsible to judge legal cases and "the implementation of contracts and orders, like the ruler of an independent state."[15] Whether the council and the ethnarch served simultaneously is unclear; a passage (*Flacc.* 74) is the basis for a theory that the council replaced the ethnarch in 12 B.C., that is, after Rome began to rule Egypt. Philo uses the Greek word *archōn* ("head," "ruler") for a member of the council, though possibly the archons were the leaders in general rather than designated members of the council. Still another title suggesting ruling authority is mentioned in Josephus,[16] that of "alabarch." Neither the office nor indeed the word itself is clear. The position was apparently one of some consequence, and it is known that it was held by Alexander Lysimachus, a brother of Philo. Alexander was eminent enough to have been the "guardian" of the mother of the Emperor Tiberius and wealthy enough to have made a substantial loan to Agrippa I. The latter was a

grandson of Herod the Great and designated as client-king of
Judea in A.D. 38. Alexander is reported to have paid for the plat-
ing of gates in the Temple at Jerusalem with gold and silver.
Assuming that there was an upper-class, wealthy segment within
the Jewish community, Philo surely belonged to it. Perhaps he
lived in a time which, though characterized by insecurity and
uneasiness, was relatively tranquil until 38. The tranquility seems
to have been permanently disturbed by the violent affairs of 38.
In the sixties the Jewish community went through upheavals,
brought on at least in part by a futile resort of some Jews to
armed violence, this in response to external pressures by hostile
Gentiles, primarily Egyptians rather than Greeks. Josephus tells
that Philo's nephew, Tiberius Alexander, used Roman soldiers to
quell the violence, reporting that 50,000 Jews were killed.[17]

The direct information about the life of the inner community
of Alexandria being so scanty, scholars have ordinarily conjec-
tured that, at least in tranquil times, what was true elsewhere of
Jewish communities about self-rule, also characterized Alexandria. Professor Erwin R. Goodenough has sought to show that
the treatises called *On the Special Laws* reflect the Jewish courts
of Alexandria[18] and, on the basis of a passage[19] in which Philo
laments that communal concerns recurrently draw him away
from his preferred quiet contemplation in his library, that Philo
had some kind of judicial role.[20] This is possible, but the fact is
that Philo does not state this unmistakenly. Indeed, he tells us
virtually nothing about himself, except about his participation in
the committee[21] sent by the Jewish community to the Emperor
Gaius Caligula in protest against the hostile failure to act on the
part of the Roman prefect Flaccus in connection with severe anti-
Jewish riots that took place in 38. Philo would scarcely have been
chosen to head the delegation to the emperor unless he was a man
of acknowledged eminence.

But we know almost nothing about his life. Also, we know
almost nothing direct about the details of his education. To have

been the brother of the wealthy alabarch implies that Philo was himself wealthy, or else had access to wealth. The leisure to write as much as he did suggests ample private means. Passages in his writings show a knowledge of how the rich live. The unmistakable learning he acquired, though we do not know where or how he did so, again suggests some measure of wealth. He mentions teachers only passingly; perhaps his thorough knowledge of Plato and other facets of Greek philosophy came from tutors. His attendance at theaters and sporting events again can be taken as evidence of financial means.

If it was only in 41, three years after the pogroms of 38, that Jews were barred by the Rescript of Claudius from enrolling in the gymnasia, then it is possible that Philo had had such schooling. The broad prohibition of such enrollment in 41 would have come too late to affect Philo. Tcherikover suggests, moreover, that it was quite possible that, even after the Rescript, individual Jews were usually able to enroll in the gymnasia. What is clear from Philo's treatise called *On Mating for the Sake of Erudition* is that he had thoroughly mastered what the gymnasia taught. The treatise, however, gives not even a hint as to how Philo achieved this mastery.

The direct information about the Jewish community of Alexandria is associated with the pogroms of 38. Philo witnessed these and then wrote about them in *Against Flaccus* and *The Legation to Gaius*. Here and there in his other treatises is a passing sentence that seems to reflect historical experience. For example, he chides the Egyptians as inhospitable, exemplified in the failure of the Pharaoh in the time of Abraham (Gen. 12:10–20) to observe the laws of hospitality. But even after one has assembled such passing sentences, the overall impression arising from his treatises other than *Against Flaccus* and *Legation* is that these treatises largely ignore anti-Semitism, either as no factor in his life or no factor in his thought. If he was married, and had begotten children, he abstains from both mention and the subtlest of clues; later legend ascribes to him a noble wife.

Repeatedly he speaks in scorn of the *ochlos*, the mob, apparently at times meaning Gentiles, but also at times meaning Jews. He speaks in scorn, too, of "literalists," those Jews who seem not to have utilized, or sympathized with, freedom and the elaborate allegory by which Philo interpreted Scripture. If he was ever invited to expound Scripture in the Alexandrian synagogue, one guesses that he bored the congregation with his erudition and wordiness quite as much as he enlightened it. Ordinary Jews would scarcely have understood his repeated citations of abstruse philosophy; if, as is sometimes thought, some of his treatises were synagogue sermons, he must have severely tried the patience of his audience.

The fragments preserved in Eusebius[22] from Greco-Jewish writers earlier than Philo are folksy in the extreme (for example, that descendants of Abraham married offspring of Hercules). Philo could scarcely have failed to know some of this literature, or to have succeeded more fully in abstaining from echoing most of it. While it is usual to view him as the pinnacle of the Greco-Jewish writings, he shows almost no direct relationship to them, except for the Septuagint, the Greek translation of the Bible. He knows, and repeats, in *Moses* II the account in the Letter of Aristeas about the origin of the Septuagint, but he otherwise ignores the whimsies of earlier Greco-Jewish writers. Philo is not greatly interested in history—a surprising matter we shall need to revert to. Philo did not possess the common touch.

What cannot be denied Philo, though, is his thoroughgoing Jewish loyalty. If at times it seems to be Judaism, rather than the Jews, to whom his loyalty is addressed, nevertheless that loyalty is beyond all denial.

Any Jewish community, whether in ancient Alexandria, or nineteenth-century Berlin, or twentieth-century Philadelphia, is

certain to present the phenomenon of apostasy. Indeed, the prelude to the Maccabean revolt of 168 B.C. was the disaffection of
the "Hellenizers" in Jerusalem from Judaism. Apostasy can be
simple or thoughtless erosion, as, for example, a by-product of a
mixed marriage; or it can be the result of succumbing to a rival,
majority civilization; or apostasy can be the device whereby a
climber feels that he can climb better. The best-known apostate
of Alexandria we have already mentioned: he was Philo's own
nephew, Tiberius[23] Alexander, the son of Philo's brother Lysimachus. Tiberius Alexander rose to become the prefect of Egypt;
under Titus, Tiberius Alexander commanded the Roman troops
in the successful assault on Jerusalem in A.D. 70. Philo tells us
nothing about apostasy in general, at least not directly; but indi-
rectly he touches on it, as we shall see. We shall see too that Philo
was quite capable of speaking with a sharpness that is not characteristic of philosophical calmness. Did such Jews on the verge of
apostasy read him? We do not know.

But if his readership was not wealthy or cultural Jews who had
absorbed and been overwhelmed by Greek culture to the point of
near apostasy, and if it was not the ordinary Jewish cobbler or
tailor, then who was it? Perhaps a sizable in-between group. We
must balance the circumstance that he was not a writer for the
masses with the fact that a great abundance of what he wrote
was copied and preserved. Philo's writings were preserved and
transmitted by Christians, not by Jews.[24] His legacy of writings
was lost to Jews (who have preserved from that age only materials in Hebrew or Aramaic and none at all in Greek). Certainly
at various stages in the early Christian centuries there were those
who thought Philo was worth preserving. In his own time, were
his followers a large group, or a small one—indeed, no more than
a coterie of fellow intellectuals? We simply do not know.

We can ascribe to him a very clear and logical mind. He also
possessed a fine memory and the capacity to correlate. His treatises, in no way models of brevity, are marked by correlations and

hence frequent repetitions. Though he ordinarily returned to a topic he was pursuing, memory and correlation furnished him with tangents which he seems to have found irresistible, especially in his treatises that are contained in the *Allegory of the Law.* One who wrote as much as Philo could readily trespass into inconsistencies. There is very little of significant accidental inconsistency in Philo. Repetitious and prone to digression though he was, Philo can nevertheless be credited with the ability to control his material; he is never controlled by it.

There is universal agreement among scholars that the Greek culture reflected in Philo is both broad and penetrating, the result of reading and study in intensity and depth. He quotes some fifty-four classical authors directly and accurately. His Greek is the *koine*, but it is in the pretentious imitation of Athens that is customarily called Atticistic.

Philo's content, even when it is Scripture he is explaining and Judaism he is defending, is always Grecian, except in one matter. In the mechanics of Philo's use of allegory—to which we presently turn—Philo gives us the translation into Greek of the Hebrew names of biblical personalities. For example, he tells us Abram is two Hebrew words, *ab* meaning father and *ram* meaning high. Abram, the *father* of the Jewish people, was born and reared in astrology, a pursuit in which the eyes are turned *high* to the heavens. So to declare that Abram means "high father" entails some knowledge of Hebrew. But apart from the etymologies of the biblical names, virtually everything else in Philo is thoroughly Grecian. Perhaps one might put things in the following way: Philo's basic religious ideas are Jewish, his intuitions Jewish, and his loyalties Jewish, but his explanations of ideas, intuitions, and devotions are invariably Greek. Scripture has its array of prophets, and Philo "believes" in prophecy; when Philo explains what prophecy is and how it works, his exposition comes from Plato.

Clearly, then, Philo was a Jew. Was he a *Greek* Jew, or, might one more properly speak of him as a Jewish *Greek?* About this topic acute controversies have taken place. The resolution of the controversies is surely an unrealizable goal, as we shall see, but a clarification of the disputed contentions is not.

# 2

## Allegory

It would be logical at this point to present the body of Philo's numerous writings, this in some systematic form. But the record of the efforts of scholars to arrange Philo's writings into some reasonable categories can present unclarity and possible misunderstanding, revolving around allegory. It is therefore desirable to precede the discussion of his writings with some remarks about allegory so that an aspect of the ensuing classification of the writings can be clear.

The basic meaning of allegory is "to say another thing." In the interpretation of sacred texts, allegory is the assertion that such texts are not saying what they are saying, but saying something different. Allegory is the direct opposite of the literal.

Allegory is a particular kind of non-literal interpretation. Philo presents a good measure of non-literal interpretation which is not presented in the form of allegory. When, in describing the journey of Abraham from Charran to Canaan, Philo says that Abraham journeyed "with only a few or even alone," he is presenting an interpretation not found in Scripture, but he is not here engaging in direct allegory. Similarly, when he interprets LXX Gen. 2:18, "It is not good for man to be alone. Let us make for him a helpmeet like him," he says, "By these words [Scripture] refers to partnership, and that not with all persons but with those who wish to help and bring mutual profit, even though they may not be able (to do so). For love is a strengthener of character, not more by usefulness than by union and concord, so that to every one of those who come together in the partnership of love, the saying of Pythagoras can be applied that 'a lover is indeed another self.' "[1] That is to say, Philo very frequently amplifies, or alters, or meditates on a scriptural passage without entering specifically into allegory.

When amplification, alteration, or meditation takes a particular form, that form is allegory. Allegory assigns a special meaning to a passage, which meaning is, on the surface, not present in the passage. For example, Philo interprets the conflict between Cain and Abel to be that of two types of persons. Cain represents the man who is fluent in speech but who is deficient in content, while Abel is the kind of man whose content is solid but whose speech is halting. A fluent man can "kill" a man of halting speech, as Cain killed Abel. There is nothing in the scriptural account that justifies this interpretation. That is normally the case with Philo's allegory.

What Philo has done in his allegorical interpretation has been to make Cain and Abel types of human beings who are to be found in every age and every place. So, throughout his writings, he transforms biblical characters, or biblical place-names, into universal types of people, or universal characteristics of mankind.

A chief purpose of allegorical interpretation is to enable one to continue to bind himself to a textual passage that is both sacred and troubling. Troubling alludes, for example, to such matters as scriptural passages which on the surface seem to be irrational, or illogical, or trivial, or tasteless. Scripture has many passages that can be troubling to a rationalistic mind, or to one who puts some premium on good taste. Is it credible that the serpent in Genesis, or Balaam's ass in Numbers, actually spoke? Again, when childless Sarah proposed that Abraham should mate with her Egyptian maid Hagar and thereby beget an heir, and Hagar thereupon became impudent to Sarah, was it proper that Abraham promptly and heartlessly acquiesced in Sarah's demand that he drive Hagar into the desert? Allegory was Philo's principal way of meeting the difficulties he found in Scripture. His allegory is very complex, and highly structured, and concerned with matters much weightier than talking animals.

Philo did not invent allegory. It is to the Stoics that scholars ascribe either the origin, or else the development, of this device. The Stoics applied this manner of interpretation to Homer and the Homeric legends. The basis of the *Iliad* was the wrath of Achilles, a wrath that arose when Achilles was compelled by the King Agamemnon to turn over to him the wench Briseis, who had been captured in a skirmish. Agamemnon had had his own Trojan wench, Chryseis, a daughter of a priest of Apollo; the god had compelled Agamemnon to restore Chryseis to her father. Thereupon Agamemnon took Achilles' Briseis, and Achilles sulked in his tent and refused to fight. What were the Achaeans doing at Troy? Trying to reclaim Helen, the wife of Menelaus, the brother of Agamemnon; Helen had run off from Menelaus with Paris, the prince of Troy. In Agamemnon's absence from home his wife Clytemnestra took a lover, Aegisthus; the two of them killed Agamemnon on his return from Troy. The sexual escapades, and the violence, were uncongenial to the Stoics. By allegory they weeded out of the Homeric legends what they deemed unseemly. Since Homer and the Bible are so different from each other, we should not expect very much in the way of an overlap in the content of Stoic and Philonic allegorical interpretation, for it was the allegorical manner that was similar and not the substance. There is, however, one preserved item wherein a Stoic allegory and a Philonic one overlap in content. It relates to the distinction that is discernible between the so-called "encyclical" studies of the gymnasia on the one hand and the true wisdom on the other. The encyclica are "preliminary" studies such as mathematics, rhetoric, or music—the forerunners of our liberal arts. Wisdom, however, is a stage beyond such preliminary studies. It was the view of both Philo and the Stoics that the student, to arrive at philosophy or wisdom, needed first to traverse the preliminary studies, since he could not get to wisdom without doing so. That there was a gradation in quality between the preliminary studies and wisdom was viewed by both as axiomatic. (In our modern educational system, while we would be prone to view the liberal arts curriculum at a university as a necessary prelude to wisdom, we would scarcely ascribe to the holder of an A.B. degree the status of having achieved wisdom. In our system, as well as in the ancient world, we would feel impelled to raise the question of just what wisdom is. Yet we would all recognize that university courses in philosophy, esthetics, and ethics are not the same in substance as wisdom—whatever definition it is that we give to wisdom. We shall later see in some detail what Philo means by wisdom.)

It is related in the *Odyssey* that Odysseus (Ulysses) had left Ithaca so as to participate in the Achaean assault on Troy. Once Troy was conquered, Odysseus went through many adventures in an immensely complicated homeward journey. Meanwhile, his noble wife Penelope was at home in Ithaca, caring for the possessions that her husband had left in her charge. For assistance, Penelope had an array of maiden servants. As the years went on, there emerged some would-be suitors eager to persuade Penelope to forget and abandon Odysseus and to yield herself to one or more of them. The character of Penelope was such that no suitor ever succeeded in making faithful Penelope his, but the maidens, on the other hand, did succumb to the seductive blandishments.[2] In the Stoic allegory, Penelope's maidens are taken allegorically to be the encyclical studies. The suitors of Penelope are the students of the encyclica. Penelope is true wisdom. The suitors, like diligent students, are able to master the maidens. Yet none is able to proceed from the mastery of the maidens to the possession of Penelope—wisdom herself.

A quite similar allegory is found in Philo. Abraham, according to Scripture, was married to Sarah, but the marriage had been childless. Sarah had an Egyptian maid, Hagar. She had proposed to Abraham that he mate with Hagar, and whatever offspring resulted would be Abraham's heir. In Philo's allegory, Abraham is at one stage the student, the man who progresses through learning. Hagar in this allegory is the encyclical studies: the student must first traverse and master the encyclical studies. Only thereafter can he proceed to a union with Sarah, who allegorically is true wisdom.[3]

The similarity in these two allegories suggests that Philo's basic method owes a partial debt both to the Stoic manner, and also to at least some of the content of Stoic allegory. In the allegory of both, the individual characters become altered into types of humans or into the characteristics of mankind.

Weird as this may seem to us, the ancient mind did not find it so at all. Rather, it was an ordinary form of understanding. In Gal. 4:24–31, when Paul wants to set forth a contention, he simply declares that what he is about to explain is an allegory.

Were there any restraints against the capricious resort to allegory? We cannot be sure. Moving to Judea, we find that the Rabbinic literature speaks of two types of interpreters, "expounders of sealed-up matters" and "expounders of difficult matters."[4] Some scholars view these expounders as allegorists along the lines of Philo, but that is disputed because it goes beyond the evidence. While allegory, unrelated to Philo's allegory, is found in Rabbinic literature, it is sporadic and without the unity found in Philo. Rabbinic tradition ascribes to the sage Hillel (who flourished just before the age of Jesus) a set of seven "norms" for interpreting Scripture, and allegory is not among them. The inference has been made that this compilation of the norms was designed to limit and exclude the far-fetched by setting forth the admissible ways of interpreting Scripture. Whether a direct purpose of the approved seven norms was to exclude allegory cannot be demonstrated. In the age after Hillel, non-literal interpretation was abundant, but allegory was not. Perhaps allegory met with disapproval by the Rabbinic sages as too extreme and too capricious.

Philo here and there alludes to "canons of allegory." He does not explain what these are; there are scholars who have tried to infer what these canons might have been and those who take the phrase "canons of allegory" to be a meaningless phrase. There is no direct discoverable relationship between the "norms" of Hillel and the "canons of allegory" of Philo.

So abundantly, almost ceaselessly, does Philo use allegory that at times the device can seem as if it is as important to the content. Philo often turns so promptly to allegory that the unwary reader may occasionally be unaware that this is happening. At times Philo simply cites some biblical character or place name without directly indicating its allegorical meaning, simply because he apparently assumes that his reader already knows. Volume I of the Loeb edition provides a brief list of biblical names and the allegorical meaning Philo ascribes to them; it can often help a beginning reader, on encountering a biblical name, to look it up in this list. In volume X of the Loeb edition (pp. 269–433) there is a much longer list, with much fuller explanations and detailed references to Philo's passages; this second list is infinitely more useful than the first.

Another aspect of Philo's interpretation is that he makes much of numbers, such as the seven branches of the sacred candelabrum or the ten sentences in the Decalogue. He proceeds to expand on the mystic nature of the particular number he chances to be discussing. There is probably no other facet of Philo's writings that to a modern reader seems quite as far-fetched as the assertions of the wondrous properties of numbers. One can discover, moreover, that Philo can call each of a variety of numbers the "most significant" of all. It is usual to ascribe this crotchet respecting numbers to the Pythagorean tradition.[5]

One word of caution to students of Rabbinic literature. There, too, certain manipulations occur respecting numbers. In both Hebrew and Greek, before the Arabic numerals were introduced, letters of the alphabet were used: aleph-alpha is one; bet-beta two, gimmel-gamma three, and so forth. Hence the Hebrew word *yd* ("hand") equals fourteen; the name Caesar Nero (*nero qesar* in Hebrew) equals 606, as in Rev. 13:18). The arithmetical tabulation of a word is called in rabbinic Hebrew *gematria*, which is a spelling in that language of "geometry."

What there is in common between gematria and Philo's caprice about numbers is limited strictly to the common supposition that there is some mystic or magic quality. The specific meanings and the processes of inference are totally divergent in the two.

To what extent Philo is himself the first Jewish adopter, the first to utilize this Stoic-like approach to Scripture, is not readily to be determined. In random passages Philo alludes to having heard the interpretations he gives from "natural philosophers." It seems reasonable that in part Philo was a legatee of a method already in existence among some Jews. Thus, certain allegories, quite different in content and tone, are found in scattered passages in Josephus[6] and in Rabbinic literature.

Assuming as we should that the method and some of the content of his allegory pre-dated Philo, to what extent did he correlate and expand the method? The answer is largely a matter of conjecture, for there is no direct evidence by which to answer the question. Yet the allegory in Philo is so thoroughly developed, and the correlation of disparate passages of Scripture made to fit into so relatively tight a unity of meaning, that one senses that these qualities are the result of a fairly long period of time and reflect not a single mind, but a sequence of them. I have elsewhere described the allegory in Philo as architectonic, meaning thereby that there is to be found a totality that indicates a completed edifice, and that the walls, the roof, and the floor and their component parts have been brought together into a unified structure. All fits together and fits together neatly.

To say this in another way, it is necessary to regard *The Allegory* in Philo as a unified entity and something quite beyond the random, disparate individual allegorical items found in Josephus or the ancient Rabbis. To repeat, the individual allegorical items in Philo all fit into what we might call his "grand Allegory."

We can in a preliminary way say the following. The grand Allegory enables Philo to transform Scripture into the nature and experience of every man. (We shall see this in greater detail in Chapter 4, "Religion in Philo.") Thus, Adam allegorically is the mind—every human has a mind—and Eve is sense perception: all minds function through the perceptions of the senses. Again, men and women differ from each other; some are bright and some stupid, some are earnest and others hypocrites. Ishmael, the son whom Hagar, the encyclical studies, bore to Abraham, is the sophist whom such studies breed. The three patriarchs, Abraham, Isaac, and Jacob, are also types of human beings.

The adhesive that binds together what Philo presents allegorically is the narrative nature of the Pentateuch. We recall that Genesis begins with the creation of the world, the creation of Adam, the loss of Eden, the generations from Adam to Noah; the flood; the generations from Noah to Abraham; the patriarchs; Joseph; the Exodus and the Wilderness, with Moses leading his people to the sacred mountain, and the revelation there of the Laws. This narration is allegorically something more than an account of the past; it is also an account of the contemporary, personal experience of every man.

It is, indeed, the spiritual journey which each one of us can make. Scripture provides the map for the journey each of us can make to spiritual perfection.

In a sense the effect of making Scripture so contemporaneous is to dissolve the history in Scripture. Philo repeatedly seems to do this. He denies that Sarah and Hagar are historical persons; he says, respecting Abraham's removal from Ur to Charran (Gen. 11:31), that we cannot possibly have any interest in some journey some man made a long time ago, unless it is a spiritual journey that we too can make.

What is this spiritual journey concerned with? We are born a mixture of body and of soul. It is in the body that the senses and passions are to be found. The soul, on the other hand, is free of evil, and, indeed, it is in the soul that the virtues potentially abide. Man's higher mind, if properly used, can so regiment the senses and passions that the soul can be freed from bodily domination. Spiritual perfection is the successful arrival by an individual to the point at which his soul is completely freed from the baleful influence of his body. The world wherein passion and the senses operate is the sensible world, our material world. There exists, though, a higher, a spiritual world, the intelligible world. He who achieves spiritual perfection, as it were, leaves this world, the sensible world, behind him and enters the lofty world of ideas, the intelligible world wherein immortality abides.

This set of two worlds is derived from Plato, and is found too in the Stoics. The sensible world (*kosmos aesthetikos*) is that of our senses, the intelligible world (*kosmos noëtos*) that of our higher minds. The senses provide *perceptions*, from which the higher mind moves on to *concepts*, to ideas.

Granting that the goal of arriving at spiritual perfection is desirable, and noble, and gratifying, the urgent question then arises: *how* does one get there? Philo gives two related answers. One is directed to men of great innate gifts (such as himself!); the other to ordinary people. Men of all ages who are by birth endowed with great innate gifts are like the patriarchs, Abraham, Isaac, and Jacob.

But how about ordinary people who do not have great gifts and who are unable to let their higher mind completely guide their actions? Such men can achieve spiritual perfection through their faithful observance of the Laws of Moses which begin in Exodus, chapter 20, and continue through the ensuing pages of the Pentateuch. God, being cognizant of man's usual limitations, mercifully provided this alternate way. The Laws of Moses are nothing other than a recording of the deeds of Abraham, Isaac, and Jacob. Whoever observes the Laws of Moses is living like Abraham, Isaac, and Jacob. There are those who faithfully observe the Mosaic laws but are without awareness that they are living like the patriarchs. This is the case with ordinary Jews whose understanding never rises above what the literal Laws set forth. But the Laws have a deeper meaning, revealed through allegory. Allegorically, circumcision prunes passion from the body. Allegorically, Passover symbolizes the passing of the soul out of domination by the body. Abstinence from pork (the "sweetest" of all meats, according to Philo) instructs in self-control. Those who fully and deeply know the allegorical meaning observe the Laws in full awareness that they are living like the patriarchs.

In describing Philo's allegory as architectonic, I mean that Philo brings the various parts of the Pentateuch, however disparate and unrelated its component parts may seem to be, into a great and good unity, a unity certainly not present on the surface. An example may clarify this. Abraham's nephew Lot had settled in the then-fertile area of Sodom. Allegorically, Lot is presumed to mean "to incline," for Lot "inclines" to physical pleasure. In this sense there is Lot in each of us, for in our progress towards spiritual perfection, we all go through a stage wherein we too incline to pleasure. Again, Lot is viewed as a stage in the progression of Abraham when the patriarch was moving forward to perfection. That is, the episodes in Scripture about Lot fit in with his overall

allegory of Abraham. Nothing at all in the Pentateuch is alien to
the allegory unified in Philo's mind.

Does Philo at times appear to strain a bit in forcing all of Scripture into this encompassing totality of allegory? In answer, he
often strains a bit, and often strains a very great deal! His use of
some biblical characters requires him to digress to justify his view
of their relationship to the unity, but he inevitably succeeds in
making the connection, however tortuous is his path to the supposed connection.

How was it that Philo decided what the allegory of particular
biblical characters and place-names should be? His method was to
state what the particular name meant in the original Hebrew and
to proceed from that meaning to his allegorical allocation. To repeat, he tells us that Abram in Hebrew means *ab*, "father," and
*ram*, "lofty." The stars are high in heaven and lofty, and Abraham is the father, the ancestor. Philo's allegorical conclusion is
that when the patriarch was Abram, that is, before his name was
altered to Abraham, he was an astrologer, having been born and
reared in astrology. If to us there are some apparently missing
steps in this identification, Philo seems untroubled by them. I de-
fer to Chapter 9 a discussion of Philo's many translations of biblical names in connection with the problem of whether or not he
knew Hebrew and how conversant or familiar he was with the
unfolding Synagogue Judaism of Judea. Here it is necessary to
say only that the determination of the allegorical meaning of biblical names is invariably buttressed by how these Hebrew names
can be translated. It is usual for Philo to give the supposed Hebrew meanings of biblical names in justifying the allegorical
meaning he assigns to them. At times the meaning he gives the
Hebrew can be judged to be correct; at times it is not. At times
he can surprise us by his view of the meaning of the Hebrew and
by his proceeding to an allegorical meaning we might not have

expected. To sum up, then, Philo utilizes the supposed meaning of the Hebrew names so as to assign an allegorical entity, and this allegorical entity deals with the names as related to the senses, or the passions, or the mind, or the soul, or to proper logic.

Philo uses allegory beyond what he can deduce from Scripture and connect with it. He also uses allegory to invest meanings he can read into Scripture so as to find there the proof for the often novel and profound insights that are his.

By resorting to the use of allegory, he is enabled to read Platonic and Stoic ideas into Scripture. But Philo would never have admitted to reading Plato into Scripture; he would have insisted that the Platonism and Stoicism came out of Scripture. He and his Christian successors assert that Philo was right because Plato derived his views from Moses, who was earlier and greater than Plato.

The end result is what should concern us, namely, that the intuitions, assumptions, and loyalties in Philo are Jewish, but the basic content of Philo's thought is Grecian. Allegory binds these together.

# 3

## Philo's Writings

It has been customary in Philonic scholarship to divide his writings into categories. This procedure is in part simply the ordinary scholarly pursuit or crotchet. In the case of Philo, the division has a purpose, namely, to try to answer the question modern scholars have raised. For whom did he write? Are some treatises addressed to Jews while others are addressed to Gentiles? This latter question arises because of the phenomenon of double treatment. If we take Abraham as an illustration, Philo devotes a number of treatises to the parts of Genesis which deal with him, for example, his treatise *Concerning the Migration of Abraham.* On the other hand, a totally different treatise, *Concerning Abraham,* repeats a large measure of what Philo has written elsewhere about Abraham. Why the double presentation?

Turning from content to external form, in *Concerning the Migration of Abraham,* Philo begins by quoting Gen. 12:1–3. The sentences, phrases, and even the words in this quotation from Scripture tend to shape the content of the treatise. The treatise in its body digresses to quote and "explain" additional scriptural passages, doing so in a way that suggests that the reader already knows this scriptural material. That is to say, in *Migration* Philo seems to assume a good acquaintance or even familiarity with the contents of Scripture.

The opposite is the case with the treatise *Concerning Abraham.* In it Philo seems to assume an unfamiliarity with biblical material on the part of the reader. He gives an account of the career of Abraham as if the reader is either totally uninformed or even in part misinformed. Moreover, *Concerning Abraham* is not preceded by a citation of a sequence of biblical verses. These differences in form and in content lead naturally to the conclusion that some of Philo's writings were addressed to an audience of the already instructed, some to the unacquainted, possibly Gentiles.

Those treatises on biblical matters that begin with a series of biblical verses, and the content of which is shaped by these verses, are known as the *Allegory of the Law.* Those treatises on biblical matters which lack an opening series of verses and the content of which flows from the title of the particular essay are known as the *Exposition of the Law.*

It should be clearly understood that the treatises in the *Exposition* are every bit as allegorical as those in the *Allegory.* Furthermore, confusion can be avoided by noticing that within the large category called the *Allegory*, there is a series of three related essays called *The Allegory of the Law!*

Some scholars arrange the Philonic corpus into six categories, some into four.[1] It is the latter arrangement that commends itself to me. But there is little at stake in whether one speaks of six categories or four.

## A. Miscellaneous Writings

The first category is often called "the historical writings." It is not a totally suitable name, for some of the works set into this category are a bit remote from history. Perhaps one might better speak of the category as "the non-biblical."

1. *Hypothetica*. The word means "suppositions," but why that should be the title is not clear. Some explain the term as implying diverse premises, with the reader at liberty to choose among these. Others, though, understand the title to mean "exhortations."[2] Hypothetica has survived only in two extracts, quoted and used by the Christian church historian Eusebius,[3] the bishop of Caesarea in Judea whose dates are 260 (?)–340 (?). In his text, Eusebius, in identifying the quotation he is about to give, speaks of "the first book of the work which he [Philo] entitled Hypothetica," where Philo is found "speaking in defense of the Jews as against their accusers." The second extract given by Eusebius speaks of a work by Philo seemingly called *Apology for the Jews*. In still another passage Eusebius, in giving a list of the works of Philo, mentions one called *About the Jews*. As F. H. Colson[4] says, "The general assumption is that these three [works] are one and the same."

The first of the two extracts is interrupted at two places by brief editorial passages from the hand of Eusebius, such as "shortly afterwards [Philo] says. . . ." The portions presented by Eusebius deal, first, with the Exodus from Egypt, handled most briefly; second, a laudatory characterization of Moses,[5] whose name chances not to appear in the portion used by Eusebius, followed by praise for the character of the Hebrews in their conquest of and settlement in the Holy Land. There ensues next what Eusebius calls a "summary of the constitution[6] laid down for the nation in the laws of Moses." The summary stresses the strictness of the Mosaic law, which makes evasions, extenuations, and postponements of punishment impossible. The obedience of wives to husbands and the responsibility of parents for the care of children are stressed. So too is the requirement to abide by even a chance utterance by which some property is dedicated to a sacred purpose. Next, Philo gives brief reflections of some "of the host of other things which belong to unwritten customs and institutions or are contained in the Laws themselves." Philo goes on to praise the Sabbath day, when Jews assemble to hear and learn the Laws; thereby all of them become well versed: "The husband seems competent to transmit knowledge of the laws to his wife, the father to his children, the master to his slaves." From the Sabbath, Philo turns to extol the Sabbath (sabbatical) year (Exod. 24:10–11; Lev. 25:2–7); the respite from cultivation of the land is comparable to the relaxations which physicians prescribe for the well.

The second extract that Eusebius provides follows a statement that the Jewish nation is divided into two parts: one, the multitudes who Moses intended should be guided by the literal meaning; two, the philosophers who rise above the literal to the higher meaning. Eusebius then reproduces the substance of *That Every Good Man Is Free*, 75–91, dealing with the Essenes, who exemplify those Jews who rise to the higher meaning of Scripture.

2. *That Every Good Man Is Free*. This treatise begins with the statement that it is a sequel to an earlier treatise, the theme of which was that "every bad man is a slave." This earlier treatise has not survived. *That Every Good Man Is Free* is often regarded as a work of Philo's youth. The substance of the treatise is an assembly of Stoic paradoxes in which virtue is always spiritual and vice always physical. The illustrations which Philo gives are predominantly from the world of Greek literature. His use of Scripture for illustrative examples is very scanty (see 43; 57; 68–69).

In the context in which Philo tells that there are small-minded men who ask for proof that there have actually been men who lived lives of spiritual purity, Philo cites some examples: the so-called "Seven Sages" of the Greek world, the Magi of Persia, and the Gymnosophists of India. He then says that Palestinian Syria has not failed "to produce high moral excellence"; the men so lauded here are the Essenes.[7] Philo lists the high attributes of the Essenes, who number 4000. Their name is a variation of the Greek word *hosiotēs*, "holiness," an allusion not to their offering of animal sacrifices, but to their resolve to sanctify the mind. The Essenes live in villages, deliberately avoiding the cities where vice is inevitable. Some are farmers, some craftsmen. They do not hoard gold or silver or acquire huge tracts of land. They neither make nor possess military weapons. They avoid commerce and its covetous drive for acquisition. They possess no slaves; they denounce slave-owners. They avoid the quibbles of the usual philosophers, retaining of philosophy only two aspects: that which treats of the existence of God and the creation of the world, and that which deals with the ethical. The latter they study industriously, "taking for their trainers the laws of their fathers which could not possibly have been conceived by the human soul without divine inspiration." On the Sabbath they gather in sacred places, which they call synagogues. They there sit decorously in rows according to their ages. One member reads aloud from the books and another, of special proficiency, expounds what is not understood. Most of their philosophical study "takes the form of allegory," thereby conforming to "past tradition."

No Essene owns private property; the doors of all their houses are open to visitors who share their convictions. They have a single treasury, common expenditures, and corporate payment for food through common meals. Out of the common treasury they care for the sick. They give great respect to elders and maintain them fully and generously.

At this point Philo adds a paragraph that is somewhat puzzling: Many rulers at various times came to power over Judea, some of whom openly outdid wild beasts in cruel savagery, while others more subtly wrought comparable evils through their impiety and inhumanity. Yet no ruler, of either category, ever laid a charge against the Essenes: "They all treated them as self-governing and freemen by nature and extolled their communal meals and [their] ineffable sense of fellowship. . . ." Is Philo here alluding to some historical circumstance? If so, no other source has survived which in any way relates to beneficent royal treatment of the Essenes.[8] Possibly it is from personal observation, for he did make at least one journey to the Temple in Jerusalem.[9] That mention of a pilgrimage to the Temple is quite incidental: Philo, speaking of the kinds of birds which Jews may or may not eat, reports, "There is a city on the seacoast of Syria called Ascalon. While I was there at a time when I was on my way to our ancestral Temple to offer up prayers and sacrifices, I observed a large number of pigeons at the crossroads. . . ."

There is nothing in the passage to imply that this was Philo's only pilgrimage to the Temple, but it is only here that we have any information of a visit to the Holy Land. Accordingly, while Philo may have personally observed the Essenes, it is not to be ruled out that he is drawing on sources or on his imagination. The latter likelihood seems strengthened by the notice of how he treats the Therapeutae in the treatise to which we now turn.

3. *On the Contemplative Life.* The full title, literally translated, is *On the Life of Vision or of Suppliants.* These suppliants, men of vision, are the Therapeutae, a monastic order which was settled near Alexandria on the shore of a lake called Mareotis.

The treatise has a subtitle: "The Fourth Part Concerning the Virtues."[10] Philo begins with an allusion to a previous writing: "I have discussed the Essenes who persistently pursued the *active* life. . . ." The Greek word rendered "active" is *praktikon;* it is balanced in Philo's next sentence by his intention now to write about those who embraced the *theorian*, meant as the opposite of praktikon.

A reliable English dictionary supports the equation of the word "contemplation" with vision; "theory" is derived from the Greek *theōrein*, to see. The contrast between the "practical" life of the Essenes and the "theoretical" life of the Therapeutae lies in the following, that the Essenes were farmers and craftsmen, but the Therapeutae apparently not. If it is asked, what did the Therapeutae contemplate, then the answer is God. Unlike the Essenes who (according to Philo, but not Josephus) were exclusively male (Josephus speaks of a group of marrying Essenes[11]), the Therapeutae had women members.

That the Therapeutae were in Philo's vicinity eliminates the acute problem of the sources of his information, but, at least for some scholars, it does not eliminate the question of the reliability of what Philo reports, as we shall see.

Indeed in a work[12] published in 1880, P. E. Lucius denied that Philo was the author of the treatise. He had two bases for his denial. One is that Eusebius, in *Ecclesiastical History* II.17, identified the Therapeutae as Christians, converted by Mark in the course of his evangelization of Alexandria. The second basis was Lucius' interpretation of a passage, #21. There Philo, while speaking of the pious who spurn the city with its evils and sojourn outside them, says that "this kind exists in many places." Since in the third century there were many Christian monastic groups, and since we know of no other such Jewish groups, Lucius incorrectly interpreted the passage to allude to Christian groups. It was also the view of Lucius that the true author was a third-century Christian who imaginatively described the monasticism of his own time, but put Philo's name on the treatise, to lend authority, and thereby authenticity, to a supposed view of the primitive church. Lucius persuaded some very eminent scholars. But in 1915 F. C. Conybeare, in his edition of *On the Contemplative Life*, confronted the issues raised by Lucius, and persuaded most scholars that Lucius' contentions about the authorship were ill-founded. The authenticity of Philo's authorship has been universally accepted. Conybeare (and others) have stressed the unmistakable Philonic character of the treatise.[13]

Apart from the issue of the genuineness of Philo's authorship, interest in the treatise has centered in the Therapeutae themselves, as one more manifestation of the varieties in Judaism in the age of early Christianity, Josephus (A.D. 37–100?) had written about the sects in Judea (Pharisees, Sadducees, Essenes, and the Fourth Philosophy[14]). The Therapeutae presumably could be added to that list, as could early Christians also.

Yet even granting that Philo could readily have known and even visited the near-by Therapeutae, it seems legitimate to raise the question of the reliability of his report, for the suspicion can arise that he is not free from idealization. His constant bent towards describing human qualities and innate personal gifts of learning, intuition, and practices as means of attaining spiritual perfection, is repeatedly reflected in the treatise; I have written elsewhere that Philo's description of the Therapeutae is consistent with his allegory, and that the latter seemingly colors his account.

*That Every Good Man Is Free* is largely a secular work, with the Jewish Essenes being introduced as little more than a passing example; *On the Contemplative Life* is primarily a Jewish work, with secular materials being introduced for contrasting examples, especially respecting some analogy between the sacred meal of the Therapeutae and the Symposium of Plato, the latter a meal accompanied by philosophical discourse.

Philo begins the treatise on the Therapeutae with an allusion to the Essenes; he says he has described them in a previous essay.[15] He then turns to a very strong assertion of the fullest reliability of what he is about to report about the Therapeutae: "I will not add anything of my own procuring to improve upon the facts . . . but shall adhere absolutely to the actual truth." One becomes suspicious that Philo "doth protest too much."

He explains the etymology of the name Therapeutae, "those who cure," in that they cure the soul, whereas city doctors cure only the body. But another possibility he offers is that the word means "worshipers," worshipers of *To On*,[16] the term Philo ordinarily uses for God. After a digression on those who worship what is not God, Philo reverts to the Therapeutae who use their "sight" to achieve the vision of God.[17]

The Therapeutae give to their children or friends their expected inheritance in advance, thus shedding wealth and property. They migrate, not into another city—all cities are filled with turmoil and vice—but to the solitude of gardens or of lonely places. The place of the Therapeutae is on a low-lying hill above Lake Mareotis. The houses there are simple; they are separate, yet near each other. Each house has a consecrated room into which the occupants take only "the laws and oracles delivered through the mouth of the prophets, and psalms" or other books which foster knowledge and piety.

The Therapeutae pray twice each day, at dawn and sunset. In between they engage entirely in *askēsis*, practice, that is, spiritual practice. "They read the Holy Scriptures," using allegory, since they think that the words of the literal text are "symbols of something whose hidden nature is revealed by studying the underlying meaning."

We should notice the continuation of this passage: "They have also writings of men of old, the founders of their way of thinking, who left many memorials of the form utilized in allegorical interpretation, and taking these as a kind of archetype, they imitate the method. . . . So, they do not confine themselves to contemplation, but also compose hymns and psalms to God in all sorts of meters and melodies. . . ."

In solitude they seek wisdom for six days, either not leaving their houses or not straying far from them. But on the seventh day (Philo abstains from saying that it is the Sabbath), they assemble, sitting in accordance to their age "in the proper attitude, with their hands inside the robe, the right hand between the breast and the chin, and the left withdrawn along the flank." Then the senior among them "who also has the fullest knowledge of the doctrines which they profess," gives in a quiet and composed voice a well-reasoned and wise discourse.

The common sanctuary (Philo does not call it a synagogue) is divided by a low wall; one side is for men and the other for women. The dividing wall is high enough to preserve the modesty of the females, but not so high as to obstruct their hearing the speaker.

During the six days they neither eat nor drink before sunset; some go without food for three days, and some for all six. On the seventh day they engage in what is sacred and festal, though they eat nothing costly: "They eat enough to keep from hunger and drink enough to keep from thirst, but abhor surfeiting as a malignant enemy to soul and body."

Presently Philo reverts to the "convivial meals"; it is his purpose to contrast the gorging in food and drink as described in Greek writings, especially in Homer, with the spiritual meals of the Therapeutae. He denounces the current "Italian expensiveness and luxury." He turns then to comment on the descriptions respectively by Xenophon and Plato of "the happily conducted banquet." Yet neither Xenophon's nor Plato's banquet is comparable to the Therapeutae's, for in Xenophon there are present "flute girls, dancers, jugglers, fun-makers"; in Plato's banquet the talk is "almost entirely concerned with love, not merely with the love-sickness of men for women, or women for men, passions recognized by the laws of nature, but of men for other males differing from them only in age."

The Therapeutae hold their meals at stated intervals.[18] They are white-robed. At a signal they form into an orderly line, with eyes and hands lifted to heaven, praying that their feasting may be acceptable to God. Women, too, share in the feast, "most of them aged virgins who have kept their chastity not under compulsion, like some of the Greek priestesses, but of their own free will in their ardent yearning for wisdom."

The men recline[19] by themselves on the right, the women by themselves on the left, not on soft couches, but on "plank beds." Not slaves (as in the case of the Gentiles) but free men, young members of the association, serve the meal. Wine is totally absent as is meat.

The president of the company then raises some question arising from Scripture, or responds to a question addressed to him. He treats the inner meaning in allegory, "for to these people the whole law book [the Five Books of Moses] resembles a living creature with the literal ordinances for its body, and for its soul the invisible meaning[20] laid up in its wording." The discourse is leisurely and is deliberately repetitious for full clarity. When it is over, there comes next a hymn, either a new one composed by the president, or an old one, of which many have been inherited in a variety of meters and melodies. Those assembled join in and chant the closing lines or refrains. It is then that the meal is served.

After the meal there are more hymns, sung by choirs respectively of men and of women, each choir being directed by a precentor. Next the two choirs join together, as in Exodus 15, where it is told that both Moses and Miriam led in hymns of thanksgiving to God for the miracle of the Red Sea crossing.

The singing continues until dawn. They turn to the east, and when they see the sun rising, they stretch their hands up to heaven and "pray for bright days and knowledge of the truth and the power of keen-sighted thinking." They then depart, each to his private sanctuary.

The more one works in Philo, the stronger is apt to arise the suspicion that the account of the Therapeutae is hardly one of restrained, accurate reporting. In recent years a variety of "communes" have arisen, and comparable idealization has seemed to me present in the glowing reports I have heard or read on the part of participants, and especially on the part of would-be participants.

4. *Against Flaccus*. This work is in a large sense historical, a review of the misdeeds of Aulus Avilius Flaccus, who was ap-

pointed Roman prefect in 32, after the Emperor Tiberius had put
the prefect Sejanus to death for his conspiratorial manipulations.
In 38 the pogroms against the Jews of Alexandria took place.

In another sense, however, the treatise could be called theological. Flaccus was recalled to Rome some time after 38. He was
then banished by the Roman authorities to the island of Andros,
and there he was executed by Roman decree, presumably in 39.
Philo wrote this treatise some time after the death of Flaccus, possibly in 41 or 42. The theological aspect of the treatise lies in its
thesis, that anyone who dares to harm the Jews is sure to come to
the same kind of dismal end that marked Flaccus.[21]

Philo begins the treatise with praise for the initial appearance
of high excellence in the administrative ability of Flaccus, the
purpose of this praise being to prepare to disclose the true villainy
of the man. The death of the Emperor Tiberius, and the designa-
tion of Gaius Caligula as the Emperor, marked the beginning of
the overt change in Flaccus; the full change came when Caligula
had put to death a certain Macro. The latter had helped Caligula
first gain and then retain the imperial throne, and was apparently
a patron of Flaccus. Flaccus underwent depression and lost his
ability to control affairs; hence he became a pawn to some power-
seekers. Philo names three of these, Dionysius, Isidorus, and
Lampo; the latter two reappear in the ensuing account. The three
were able to manipulate Flaccus on the basis that he required
an intercessor to propitiate Caligula. That intercessor would be
the city of Alexandria itself. Were Flaccus to damage the Jews, the
intercession would be the more effective. Flaccus accepted the
suggestion.

An open manifestation occurred after Caligula had designated
Herod Agrippa I as king of Judea. Agrippa was then in Rome.
Gaius proposed that the route Agrippa should follow to Judea
include a stop at Alexandria. On his arrival at Alexandria, Agrippa
disembarked quietly at night to visit "his host."[22]

The associates of Flaccus contended that the visit by Agrippa to Alexandria could undermine the position and prestige of Flaccus. The latter acted correctly to Agrippa, but only out of fear of Caligula. Yet he permitted "the lazy and unemployed mob" to vilify Agrippa in theatrical farces.[23] In not halting this vilification, Flaccus in effect was a party to it.

The mob proposed to install images in the synagogues (for which Philo here uses the term *proseuchē*). This, says Philo, was illegal. Despite the great Jewish population of Alexandria and Egypt, and the awareness that any desecration of the synagogues was an attack on all the Jews, Flaccus sanctioned the installation of the images. Such action in Alexandria could lead evil people to do the same everywhere, "for so populous are the Jews that no one country can hold them, and therefore they settle in very many of the most prosperous countries in Europe and Asia, both in the islands and on the mainland."

Philo asserts that to destroy synagogues was to deprive Jews of the opportunity of paying homage to Caesar. To disturb ancestral customs, outrage fellow citizens, and teach the inhabitants of other cities to disregard the claims of fellow-feeling was without honor.

But Flaccus proceeded even beyond the seizure of synagogues. He went on to denounce Jews as foreigners and aliens, thereby depriving them of their rights as citizens. In the ensuing violence, Jews were forced out of four of the five sections of Alexandria where they lived into a single section. Their houses and shops were pillaged, thereby impoverishing them. But even beyond that, Jews were physically beaten, and some were killed, and others burned to death.

The respected *gerousia* ("council of elders") of the Jewish community was not immune. Thirty-eight of its members were arrested, compelled to march in procession in the marketplace, and then stripped and lacerated with scourges, so that some died at once and others were long incapacitated. Some were crucified, and Flaccus abstained from having their bodies cut down for the relatives to bury. All this took place at a period in which the Emperor's birthday fell. Normally, respect for the occasion would have brought about the postponement of legal punishment; Flaccus instead used the occasion for illegal actions. On the allegation that Jews had stocks of weapons in their houses, Flaccus had his soldiers fruitlessly search Jewish homes.

Philo then introduces (a bit out of order) the maltreatment of Jewish women who, as the price for release from arrest, were compelled to eat swine flesh.

A message of birthday congratulations which the Jewish community had wished to send to the Emperor Caligula was held up by Flaccus, this so as to imply to the Emperor that Jews alone were hostile to him. When Herod Agrippa was in Alexandria, he was told of this matter; he promised to inform Caligula of the Jewish effort to congratulate him.

At this point in the treatise (#104), Philo says that justice has now entered in against Flaccus. Normally when a governor's term was over, on his return to Rome, he had to render an account to the Emperor, particularly when aggrieved cities sent ambassadors to Rome to complain. In the case of Flaccus, however, a company of soldiers came to Alexandria and arranged to arrest him in such a way that he could not flee. The blow which fell on Flaccus, Philo writes, "was caused, I am convinced, by his treatment of the Jews." The arrest came at the Feast of Booths, the celebration of which had been made impossible.

When Flaccus was brought to Rome, he discovered that his erstwhile allies, Isidorus and Lampo, were there to make serious charges against him, including some that were without foundation. In due time Flaccus was deprived of his property, sentenced to be banished to "the most miserable of the Aegean islands, named Gyaros." He was actually exiled to the island of Andros, after an intercession on his behalf. On his journey to Andros, he faced public reproaches in many places he had to traverse. Held in seclusion in Andros, he lost his reason, for he knew that the furies would avenge the wrongs he had done to the Jews.

Finally, Caligula sent emissaries to execute Flaccus. Flaccus in vain tried to escape. The butcheries which his executioners wrought on his body were as numerous as the number of Jews he had unlawfully put to death.

F. H. Colson[24] expresses the judgment that "those who admire the beauty and spirituality so often shown [in Philo's biblical treatises] might well wish [this treatise] to have been left unwritten." The tone of Philo's gratification at the downfall of Flaccus is surely vindictive. But is it reasonable to suppose that anyone who lived through the events described would fail to respond as Philo to the downfall of the oppressor? Colson's comment was published in 1941. Presumably the words were written in 1940 or even earlier, well before the Battle of Britain which Colson may have witnessed.[25] I wonder whether Colson is not here a bit callous about the vicissitudes which the Alexandrian Jews experienced, and his judgment not too harsh, considering the circumstances.

5. *The Legation to Gaius*. Like *Against Flaccus*, this treatise is both historical and theological. Respecting the historical, it reviews events in Alexandria which led the Alexandrian Jews to send an embassy to Rome; it recounts what the embassy there encountered. As to the theological, the treatise begins with the thesis that men are prone to judge the present blindly; they are unaware of God's providence and of his care for his people Israel. The treatise terminates in some confusion, for Philo speaks at the end of his obligation to proceed to the "palinode." This "balancing" or "reversing" conclusion would presumably have told of the violent death of Caligula, just as the last part of *Against Flaccus* describes the reversal of the latter's fortunes. If Philo did write such a palinode to *The Legation*, it did not survive, and is not

mentioned by Eusebius who might have done so had it been there.

The treatise is quite long and our review must omit some items. Much of it (8–113) is an account of the character and personality of Caligula, allowing Philo to pour scorn on Caligula's pretensions to being a god, and to brag that while all the Empire succumbed to Caligula's deification of himself, only the Jews declined to do so, this out of their monotheistic scruples.

The rabble of Alexandria took advantage of the disfavor of the Jews in the eyes of Caligula to perpetrate cruel and illegal deeds (set forth here more briefly than in *Against Flaccus*). The mob installed images of Caligula in the synagogues; in the largest and most notable synagogue they put a bronze statue of a man, mounted on a chariot. Previously, none of the ten or more kings of the Ptolemaic line had ever had images of themselves put into synagogues, nor had Caligula's predecessor, the Emperor Tiberius, in his twenty-three year reign, done so, nor had Augustus Caesar in his forty-three year reign.

Yet quite beyond such desecration of Alexandrian synagogues was Caligula's command to Petronius, the procurator of Judea, to set a statue of Zeus in the Temple at Jerusalem (Caligula had proclaimed himself as Zeus "made manifest"). Petronius, having informed the Jews of this intention, was greatly alarmed at the responsive uproar which would come from Jews throughout the world; at the same time he was fearful of not carrying through the command of the Emperor. His way out of the dilemma was to advise Caligula that he would comply with the command but that some delay was prudent.

At that juncture, Herod Agrippa I came to Rome. He knew nothing of the command of Caligula to Petronius nor of the written advice of Petronius. When face to face with Caligula, the latter expressed his displeasure that the Jews would not acknowledge him as a god and that they had obstructed his command about installing the statue of Zeus in the Temple. Agrippa fell into a faint, and, unconscious, needed to be carried away.

After about a week in a coma, Herod Agrippa recovered enough to write a long letter to Caligula, which Philo reproduces. In it he stressed the centrality of Jerusalem and the Temple in world-wide Jewry. Agrippa commented that Jerusalem was the first of the eastern cities to address Caligula as emperor. Caligula's grandfather, Agrippa, had visited the Temple; Augustus Caesar had honored and sanctioned its support. Even ill-disposed people would never dream of setting up an image in the Temple.

A digression in Herod Agrippa's letter denounces Pontius Pilate (procurator during the public career of Jesus, and a figure in the Gospels). Pilate had outraged the populace by dedicating for Herod's palace some shields coated with gold. Pilate, "naturally inflexible, a blend of self-will and relentlessness," stubbornly refused to take down the shields. The Jews threatened to report the matter to Rome, to the Emperor Tiberius. Pilate feared that the Jews would report to Rome in full "the briberies, the insults, the robberies, the outrages and wanton cruelties, the executions without trial constantly repeated." But Pilate did not have the courage to take down the shields. When Tiberius was informed about the shields, he rebuked Pilate in violent anger and bade him to remove the shields at once (and to install them in the Roman temple in Caesarea). The precedent of the matter of the shields in the palace surely pointed the way for the weightier matter of the image in the Temple.

The letter of Herod Agrippa goes on to rehearse more details of Roman goodwill to the Temple. Near its conclusion, Herod Agrippa writes, "Either I must seem a traitor to my people or no longer be counted as your friend as I have been." Caligula then reluctantly sent word to Petronius to abstain from further steps to violate the Temple.

Caligula, says Philo, was both untrustworthy and changeable. Though he cancelled the desecration of the Temple, he "took possession of the synagogues in the other cities after beginning with those of Alexandria, by filling them with images and statues of himself in bodily form" (the latter defining what is meant by "made manifest").

Earlier in the treatise (180–184), Philo tells that Caligula had at first received the delegation, along with the hostile Alexandrians, with the words, "I will hear your statement of the case myself when I get a good opportunity." Philo's associates rejoiced "as though we had already won the case." His own contrary view, in virtue of his age and possession of better sense, led to his being upset. The words of Caligula seemed to him to be addressed to the hostile Alexandrians present, not to the Jews: "Thus thinking, I was deeply disturbed and had no rest by day or night."

The so-called hearing was hostile and almost farcical. The foe of the Jews, Isidorus, spoke against them; the Jews spoke in refutation. Meanwhile Caligula was at this time surveying the houses in the gardens where he was then staying, inspecting the chambers and rooms. Philo writes that, after giving some orders about the houses, "He put to us this grave and momentous question, 'Why do you refuse to eat pork?'" Those of his entourage present burst into great laughter. When shortly thereafter the Jewish delegation began to speak about citizenship, this "in a manner by no means contemptible," Caligula interrupted and "dashed at high speed into the large room to give orders about its windows." He reverted to the Jews, asking, "What is it that you say?" Presently Caligula said that the Jews "seem to be people unfortunate rather than wicked. . . ." Then he terminated the hearing.

Philo, in concluding the treatise, ruminates that it was "a cruel situation that the fate of all the Jews everywhere should rest on us five envoys." He then ends with the words that he "must also describe the palinode."

Gaius Caligula died, being murdered by one Cassius Chaerea in 41. Caligula was to become notorius in the accounts by Roman historians, who charged him with both extreme tyranny and insanity, the latter based on his demand to be recognized as a god.

Without the palinode, Philo's treatise ends abruptly and inde-
cisively. If the conjecture by scholars is right that in the palinode
Philo described how divine retribution overtook Caligula, then the
purpose of the treatise becomes all the more intelligible.

## B. The Exposition of the Law

1. *On the Life of Moses.* In turning to the second category,
*The Exposition of the Law*, briefly characterized above, the
two-part treatise, *On the Life of Moses*, might be here treated
first, this for the reason that possibly it does not belong within
this category; it was the view of Erwin R. Goodenough that
*On Moses* was written for Gentiles, with a purpose beyond
the merely apologetic, namely, as a conversionist effort.[26] If the
*Exposition* as a totality was written for friendly Gentiles, the
direct missionary purpose of *On Moses* would be a reasonable
theory. The first difficulty with the theory is that of ascertaining
just who the "friendly Gentiles" were. Victor Tcherikover has
demonstrated to the satisfaction of most scholars that there is no
evidence that Gentiles (as distinct from Christians) read any
Jewish writings, whether the Septuagint or Philo. Accordingly,
the supposition that the direct purpose of *On Moses* was to convert Gentiles seems a bit extreme.

Yet an obliquely related missionary purpose is tenable, especially if we conceive of the presence in Alexandria of Jews nearly
on the verge of leaving the Jewish community, as did Philo's
nephew; *The Exposition* might well have been addressed to them.
After publishing this as a possibility, I have met acquiescence with
it in a number of scholarly writings. However, there could conceivably be very little difference in actuality in the tone of a
writing whether it was aimed at friendly Gentiles or at uninformed Jews on the threshold of apostasy.

The treatise *On Moses* is divided into two distinct parts. *On
Moses* I (as Philo states explicitly at the beginning of *On Moses*

II) is a rather straightforward retelling of the biblical narrative, and is mostly free of allegory. Philo says that it is his "hope to bring the story of this greatest and most perfect of men to the knowledge of such as deserve not to remain in ignorance of it. . . . While the fame of the laws . . . has traveled throughout the civilized world . . . the man himself . . . is known to few."[27] Philo will base his account both on what can be read in Scripture and on what he has heard "from some elders of the nation."[28] Accordingly, Philo adds material to what is in Scripture[29] (as did the ancient Rabbis and Josephus).

In his leisurely way in *On Moses* I, Philo retells the scriptural narrative with both significant additions and omissions. Unlike Scripture, which is quite laconic and devoid of the exploration of the inner psyche,[30] Philo is quite discursive and very prone to explore the inner minds of his characters. Indeed it is no overstatement to suggest that his portrait of Moses uses the biblical account primarily as a point of departure for his own purposes. Thus, for example, his recasting of Exod. 3:13–15 and the words "I am what I am," is the point of departure for his view, also expressed elsewhere (for example, in *On the Change of Names,* 11 ff.), that God is actually nameless; men in their weakness seek some title for God, and hence God is "the God of the three men whose names express their virtue. . . . Abraham by being taught, Isaac by nature, Jacob by practice." This interpretation of the patriarchs occurs again and again in Philo's writings.

There is an omission from *On Moses* I that seems deliberate: the Sinai episode does not appear in the narrative. It appears, however, in *On Moses* II, seemingly being deferred in conformity with Philo's overall purposes. He writes at the beginning of Part II that Moses, "through God's providence, became king and lawgiver and high priest and prophet." By implication Part I dealt with Moses as king, that is, as the philosopher-king, in the Platonic[31] sense. Philo in *On Moses* I, 162 and II, 4 associates with that role a Stoic doctrine that a proper king was a *nomos empsy-*

*chos kai logikos,*" a law incarnate and made vocal." (We shall need to return to this matter.)

Having dealt in Part I with Moses as the philosopher king, Philo in Part II deals with the other three offices, lawgiver, high priest, and prophet. Since Moses, in addition to these offices, was the author of the Pentateuch, he divided his writings into two parts: one part the historical, and the other the legislative (*On Moses* II, 45–47). Philo goes on to say that one section of the historical part deals with the creation of the world, the other section with particular persons. The treatises in *The Exposition* which are "historical" include *On the Creation of the World;* examples of particular persons are *On Abraham,* and *On Joseph.* If Philo wrote treatises on Isaac and Jacob, as seems likely, these did not survive.

As to the second division, namely, the legislative, these treatises are *On the Decalogue,* and the four-part *On the Special Laws,* and *On the Virtues.* That is to say, Philo reflects in *On Moses* II a basic scheme of what binds together the treatises that comprise *The Exposition.*

Reverting now to the matter of the Sinai episode, a further word in preface is here needed. Philo asserts that Moses never commands, never issues orders; rather, he suggests and admonishes. It is Philo's overall contention that the Mosaic laws rest on what for the moment we might call reason. Commands and orders, being forces outside man, are inconsistent with the view that the Mosaic laws rest on reason, since reason is inner to man. Accordingly, the Sinai episode is necessarily so treated that Philo's stress is on internal reason, not on external arbitrary commands. The account of the Sinai episode in *On Moses* II (66 ff.) is within the section devoted to Moses as priest. To function as priest, Moses had to be clean, in both soul and body; he therefore abstained from eating, drinking, and sexual intercourse. Prepared through this abstention, "he ascended an inaccessible and pathless mountain, the highest and most sacred in the region." After forty

days there, "Moses descended with a countenance far more beautiful than when he ascended"; the people could not stand "the
dazzling brightness that flashed from him like the rays of the
sun."[32]

Philo then presents in the treatise the cult matters (the produc-
tion of the Tabernacle, its vessels and the like) found in the latter
part of Exodus, in Leviticus, and in Numbers.

As to the Tabernacle, the Deity is portrayed in Exod. 25:9, as
instructing Moses to make it "in accordance with the pattern"
which the Deity will show Moses. The supposition of a divinely
revealed pattern is repeated in Exod. 25:40, 26:30, and 27:8. As
we might expect, Philo equates the divinely conceived pattern
with the Platonic "idea"; what ensues in material form is the
substitution for, or imitation of, the idea.

Rationalist that he is, Philo omits much more from his presentation of the biblical account of the Sinai episode than he relates
(such as the heavenly pavement and the sight of the Deity, Exod.
24:9–11). The Sinai episode for Philo is essentially an unique example of the achievement of Moses through his reason, rather
than only a supernatural intervention and revelation of laws on
the part of the Deity.

This is borne out when Philo turns to discuss Moses as a
prophet "of the highest quality" (*On Moses* II, 188). Philo does
not at all deny the capacity of Moses to predict the future. He
declares that there are three kinds of divine utterances: one kind
is that which God in his own person speaks, with the prophet
being the interpreter; a second is the result of question and answer; a third is that "spoken by Moses in his own person, when
possessed by God and carried away out of himself." Philo gives
several biblical examples of the latter two kinds, this bearing out
the capacity of Moses to predict what is shortly to happen; indeed, the clinching argument in support of Moses' ability to predict the future is his description while still alive of his impending
death and burial and the month-long mourning for him (Deuter-

onomy, chapter 34). According to Philo, at the point where
Moses was "to make his pilgrimage from earth to heaven, and
leave this mortal life for immortality," God altered him from his
two-fold nature of soul and body into a single unity, making his
whole being into mind. Philo does not present in clear explicit-
ness in *On Moses* what he does in various passages of *The Allegory* that allegorically Moses is pure mind; here he does so only
implicitly. As law-giver, Moses was "the best of all law-givers in
all countries"; "his laws are most excellent and truly come from
God." Moses is alone in that his laws are "firm, unshaken, immovable" and "stamped, as it were, with the seals of nature[33]
itself."

Philo now feels called upon to comment on the circumstance
that he and the other Alexandrian Jews utilized not the original
Hebrew (Philo says "Chaldean"), but the translation into Greek.
How, in view of the defects usually inherent in a translation,
could the Mosaic Laws as found in the Greek be regarded as
firm, unshaken, and immovable? Philo answers the question by
repeating the substance of the account of the origin of the Greek
translation as related in The Letter of Aristeas. Philo offers some
embellishment of his own. The account in The Letter of Aristeas
tells that Demetrios of Phaleron, the librarian, had lamented to
Ptolemy Philadelphus that the great library at Alexandria lacked
the Pentateuch. With the sanction of Ptolemy Philadelphus,
Demetrios had invited to Alexandria seventy-two priests of Jerusalem who knew Greek as fluently as they knew Hebrew. In
Philo's version,[34] Demetrios goes unmentioned; the credit is ascribed solely to the Ptolemy. Also, in Philo's version, the translators found a suitable isolated place on the island of Pharos. Gathered there, they held the sacred books in hands stretched out to
heaven, asking God that they not fail in their purpose. Then,
"they became as it were possessed and, under inspiration,[35] wrote,
not each scribe something different, but the same word for word,
as though dictated by an invisible prompter." As a result, "if

Chaldeans have learned Greek, or Greeks Chaldean, and read both versions . . . they regard them with awe and reverence as sisters. . . . [They] speak of the authors not as translators but as prophets and priests and prophets of the mysteries."[36]

This acclamation of the Greek translation seems a bit defensive. One can speculate that Philo had encountered some aspersions of the Greek translation by Judean visitors to Alexandria who boasted of their superiority in that they possessed and used the Hebrew original. Hence the defensiveness.[37] But beyond the possibility of defensiveness, Philo needed to acclaim the Greek version in order to justify his conviction that in it and through it, he was in fullest touch with the divine, being in full accord with its author, Moses, pure mind.

The four offices of Moses are significant, not alone because they characterize Moses himself, but because they delineate the role of Scripture in that it was for Philo a living, contemporaneous writing. His praise in the treatise is for the man Moses, but that is in reality his way of portraying his veneration of Scripture.

Again respecting the question, for whom was *On Moses* written, in one passage (II, 44), Philo comments that the Jewish people "are not flourishing. . . . But, if a fresh start should be made to brighter prospects . . . each nation [in the world] would abandon its peculiar ways, and, throwing overboard their ancestral customs, turn to honoring our laws alone." Earlier (II, 25) he says that "the sanctity of our legislation has been a source of wonder not only to the Jews but also to all other nations. . . ." Such passages, and other similar ones, readily suggest that Philo here is writing for Gentiles. Yet it is just as likely that he is appealing to half-assimilated Jews, arguing that since outsiders could have so high a regard of Judaism, there is reason for half-assimilated Jews to do the same.[38]

2. *On the Creation of the World.*[39] The treatise rests on the account of creation at the very beginning of Scripture, that is, in

Genesis, chapter 1. The treatment is largely Platonic and, as commentators have noted, owes a debt to Plato's Timaeus. Two themes, which one might call Jewish, recur in the treatise. One is that God created the world out of nothing. That is to say, there did not pre-exist some matter, some material, which God, at creation, utilized, shaping it into the form of the world.[40] The Aristotelian view held that the world was without beginning and was everlasting. Such a view, on the one hand, in effect negates creation, which implies a beginning; on the other hand, if the world is everlasting, in effect God's control of the world is negated, for just as God began the world, so also he had the power to end it (7-13). If God lacks such power, in effect he is no longer active, but is passive. In principle, then, a belief in the creation needs to be balanced by the possibility of the destruction of the world.

As to the second theme, granted that the world is not necessarily everlasting and is destructible, God exercises his providence on behalf of the world. Thereby, on the one hand, the world is cared for, and, on the other hand, God is shielded from the impious notion that, after creation, he simply became passive. Accordingly, creation and providence are themes which tend to shape this treatise.

Significantly, Philo begins the treatise by bringing creation into relationship with the Laws of Scripture. The specific laws, it will be recalled, appear for the first time in Exodus, chapter 20. Moses the lawgiver "refrained, on the one hand, from stating abruptly what should be practiced or avoided, and on the other hand . . . from inventing myths himself or acquiescing in those composed by others."[41] Creation by God, so Philo asserts, signifies that the world is in harmony with the Law and the Law with the world. Because of this harmony, the man who observes the Law "is constituted thereby a loyal 'citizen of the world,' regulating his doings by the purpose and the will of 'nature.' " Here Philo is reflecting Stoic ideas: by "nature" Stoics meant the very basic and highest elements of existence; a "citizen of the world" was one who lived not by the laws of his country, which were possibly unjust or inadequate, but by the highest requirements innate in the structure of things. (We shall return to this idea of "nature.") That is to say, the account of creation at the beginning of Scripture is a necessary preface to the Laws which appear later on in Exodus, the second book of Scripture.

Consistent with both Platonic and Stoic dualism, Philo speaks here, and throughout his writings, of the distinction between the perceptible or the sensible world (*kosmos aesthetikos*), that is, the world which the senses (sight, hearing, and the like) can encounter, and the world of concepts, the intelligible world (*kosmos noētos*) which the mind, proceeding from and beyond the senses, can encounter. The creation in Genesis relates to the sensible world. What is in the sensible world is subject to constant change as is everything material; what is in the intelligible world, the world of concepts, being immaterial, abides in a constant state. The details of the account of creation in Genesis, chapter 1, now serve to enable Philo to set forth his views of the relationship between the sensible world to the events there depicted. He makes special use of the numbers, that is, the six days of creation, and the acts of creation allocated to these days each by number, calling into use a developed use of Pythagorean concern about numbers. This complex material need not here be summarized. Rather, we should note Philo's view that when God was minded "to found the *megalopolis*, the 'one great city'"—another allusion to the universe as an inherent unity—"He conceived beforehand the models of its parts," and then went on to bring to completion a world discernible to the senses. As to the *kosmos noētos*, it "would have no other location than Divine Reason (*theios logos*)."

The first man (belonging in the intelligible world) was created perfect in soul and in body. His descendants (in the sensible world) preserve some marks of kinship to the perfect first man: "Every man, in respect of his mind, is allied to the Divine Reason, having come into being as a copy or fragment or ray of that blessed nature [the Divine Reason], but in the structure of his body he is allied to all the world. . . ."

Philo uses the Eden story to illustrate how pleasure [the serpent] worked on the senses [Eve] to blunt the mind [Adam].[42] (In other passages, Eden represents generic[43] Virtue; the trespass in Eden was man's loss of Virtue.)

Philo closes the treatise with a statement of the five principal doctrines which Moses has taught: one, the eternal existence of God, this in refutation of atheists; two, the unity of God, this against polytheists; three, the world came into being and is not eternal; four, the world is a unity; five, through Providence, God cares for the world.[44]

3. *Concerning Abraham.* This treatise, as Philo says at its beginning, follows directly on *On Creation.* The treatise has in the Greek a long title, presently to be mentioned. Some prefatory words are here needed. The goal of the *Exposition* seems to be to lead the reader on to ensuing treatises, particularly to *On the Decalogue* and *On the Special Laws.* An issue for Philo (and other Greek Jews) was the peculiarity that the title given in the Greek translation of the Pentateuch was that of *Nomos,* the *Law.* But Genesis is a book of narratives, not of laws. How, then, can Genesis fit logically in a work called the *Law?* The answer that Philo gives rests on his distinction between the "special laws," that is, specific, written requirements, and the so-called Unwritten Law of Nature. By the latter, Philo, using Stoic categories, means ideal law, existing in the *kosmos noëtos;* the specific, written laws are imitations of or substitutes for the Unwritten Law of Nature. (Just as the idea of a table can be imitated in a physical, wooden table, so the Unwritten Law of Nature can be imitated in the legislation of a human senate of a city-state or in the decrees of a tyrant.) The Unwritten Law, being ideal, is perfect; the written laws, being material, can fall short of perfection, and usually do,

as in the case of Athenian or Spartan law. The full title of the treatise is, *"The Life of the Sage Made Perfect Through Instruction, or the First Book of the Unwritten Laws, Which Is About Abraham."*

This treatise provides a continuation of the theme at the beginning of *On Creation,* where we saw that Philo argues for a direct connection between creation and the Laws. The continuation here takes the form of showing the direct connection between the narratives of Genesis and the Laws to be encountered in Exodus. Besides this treatise on Abraham, it is a reasonable conjecture, generally accepted by scholars, that Philo also wrote treatises on Isaac and Jacob, especially in the light of the words "First Book." These treatises on Isaac and Jacob have been lost. Assuming there were these three books on the Unwritten Law, these plus the treatise *On Joseph* constitute what Philo calls the "historical," as distinct from the "legislative," and they serve as a bridge between *On Creation* and *The Special Laws.*

Philo sets forth that he will proceed "in regular sequence"; hence, he will postpone his consideration of the particular laws which are only copies, and examine first "those which are more general and may be called the originals of these copies." Philo goes on to explain: the particular laws (which begin in Exodus, chapter 20) are "nothing else than memorials" of the lives of the patriarchs found in Genesis. The patriarchs lived in accordance with the Unwritten Law of Nature; the particular laws set forth as requirements for their descendants those deeds which the patriarchs did. Not only is Philo here straining to show in what sense Genesis properly belongs in a book of *law,* but he is also solving a problem inherent in Scripture. That problem is the relationship of the patriarchs who lived before the age of Moses to the laws that arose during the career of Moses, their descendant. This problem also claims the attention of Jubilees, the ancient Rabbis, and Paul. The solution in Jubilees and the Rabbis is to regard the patriarchs as pre-Mosaic observers of the Mosaic Laws;

in this solution, the Laws of Moses are the assumed norm, and the patriarchs are raised to it. In Philo (and in Paul), the patriarchs are regarded as the norm, and the Mosaic Laws need to be brought into conformity with the patriarchs.

Consistent with Philo's view that Genesis belongs within The Law on the basis that it is the book of the Law of Nature, the patriarchs are each a *nomos empsychos kai logikos* (as above, pp. 48–49, Moses was also). The idea in the phrase is related to Hellenistic notions of kingship and to the broader question of what philosophically makes a law truly legal, as distinct from a capricious or tyrannical edict which can in reality be "illegal." A philosopher-king, who rises out of bodily impediments, can let his higher mind soar up into the ether and there absorb the Unwritten Law of Nature. Such a philosopher-king is an embodiment of law (a *nomos empsychos*) and whatever he does is legal law. When such a monarch issues a decree, that decree thereby becomes articulated. Edwin R. Goodenough has translated the phrase by "a law incarnate and made vocal," the last word meaning "articulated," whether orally or in writing. Colson translates the phrase as a law "endowed with life and reason." Neither translation seems to me fully apt, but each conveys the general Stoic idea about a man of highest worth whose deeds are worth emulating because they represent the highest norms that a man can reach.

The patriarchs attained the eminence of being incarnate laws through the endowments with which, through God's grace, they were born. All men are born with endowments, though these may well be less than those of the patriarchs. Some men are so richly endowed that they are potentially kindred to and even equal to the patriarchs; other men, less well endowed, can aspire only to imitate the patriarchs. Ordinary Jews, lacking rich endowments, imitate the patriarchs through the medium of observing the Mosaic Laws. So much for the moment, though there is more to be said later.

Philo, in our context, has said that the more general laws must precede the specific, and that the patriarchs are these more general laws. He turns now to some of the material in Genesis which ensues after creation and which precedes the mention of Abraham in Gen. 11:26. Philo is here very selective, concentrating briefly on three persons: Enos (Gen. 4:26); Enoch (Gen. 5:21–24); and Noah (Gen. 6:8ff). Enos (which in Hebrew means "man") is epitomized in the word "hope"; in the Septuagint of Gen. 4:26, the reading[45] with respect to Enos is "this one hoped to call on the name of God." Hope, says Philo, is the first step towards the possession of blessings. (Mankind, it is to be recalled, has already lost Eden, generic virtue, and hence could have wallowed in despair.)

The second place, after hope, is repentance, symbolized by Enoch.[46] His "translation" is taken to be moral, and hence the identification of him with repentance. Noah means "rest" or "tranquility" in Hebrew. Perhaps our modern phrase "peace of mind" suggests what Philo has in mind: hope leads to repentance and repentance to peace of mind. The latter is not and cannot be mankind's ultimate goal; Noah, according to Scripture (Gen. 6:9), was righteous "in his generations," and these words mean that Noah was righteous only when compared with his contemporaries. His righteousness was therefore at best relative, and did not equal that of the patriarchs or Moses.

Tranquility, to repeat, is not the ultimate goal, but a prerequisite for further progression. The latter entails the use of man's innate endowments, which number three: the capacity to learn, intuition, and practice.[47]

Man's possible capacities or endowments are presented in Scripture in the patriarchs, Abraham representing instruction, Isaac intuition, and Jacob practice. The historical patriarchs reached perfection because each of them possessed all three endowments, but each was especially marked by that one of the three which predominated in him. Enos, Enoch, and Noah yearned for virtue; the patriarchs actually achieved it.

The endowments which characterize the patriarchs bring it about that the patriarchs allegorically are the endowments themselves; that is, there is an Abraham in us, an Isaac in us, and a Jacob in us. These innate endowments are called "the Graces," because they are God's gracious, free gift to men. The patriarchs are the three types of endowment "rather than actual men" (#54). The patriarchs are the forebears of the nation, known in Hebrew as Israel, which means "He who sees God." "Sees" is not here meant to be perception by the eyes, but by the mind; such "sight" is the highest point to which man can advance.

All that has so far appeared in the treatise is the prelude to Philo's presentation of Abraham. In the structure of what follows, the Abraham material is divided into two parts. First comes Abraham's "piety," that is, his relationship to God (60–207); second, his possession of the four virtues which describe his relationship to man.[48] The four are the Stoic cardinal virtues: justice, bravery, prudence, and temperance (208–276). This presentation of piety on the one hand, and of the virtues on the other, also marks the structure of *On the Decalogue*.[49]

In the section on piety, Philo is true to his identification of Abraham with instruction in that he tells us what it was that Abraham learned, as will presently unfold. The treatise is in effect an epitome, or even a digest, of Philo's total philosophical outlook, encompassing his view of God, the intermediaries between God and man, and man's capacity to rise to God. God, as we have said, is *To On*, "the Truly Existing," and is beyond man's reach. The intermediaries are here presented (based on Gen. 18:1, that Abraham "raised his eyes and saw three men") as three, the Logos, the Power (dynamis) of creation and the Power of Rulership.

To understand what Philo means, we must turn things about as he himself does, namely, to notice that with respect to knowing

about God, men vary in their ability. The lowest category is that
of men who do not rise above the capacity to know that the
world was created; all men are capable of seeing that the world
exists. When Scripture uses the word *Theos*, that alludes to
"God" as the creator. Creation is a Power in the sense that God
is more than merely the creator; a Power is a single facet of God
who is marked by many powers.

A category of man higher than those who are limited to recognizing the Creator is the category of those who can recognize
that God rules the world. When Scripture used the word *Kyrios*,
"Lord," this is an allusion to the Power of ruling the world. Thus,
the sun always rises in the east and sets in the west, and the seasons
follow each other in regularity, spring following winter, and
summer spring. The man who can discern God's Rulership is
higher than the man who only discerns God's Creation.

These two categories of men are in the domain of what the
senses of man can perceive, that is, they are in the sensible world.
The category above these is those who rise beyond perception
through the senses, and move into the domain of the reasoning
capacity of man. The possession of the capacity for reason leads
man into the *kosmos noëtos*, the intelligible world, there to encounter the Divine Logos. So to encounter the Logos through
reason is superior to discerning the Powers through the senses.
The three visitors to Abraham are the Logos, the Power of Creation, and the Power of Rulership. The "triple vision" is in reality
single, for the three, the Logos and the two Powers, reflect the
unity of God, a unity that transcends all other kinds of unity.

The Divine Logos—a subject to which we return in Chapter
5—is the upper limit of man's possible attainment in his moving
toward God, even by a richly endowed mind because God by
axiom is beyond man's capacity. On the other hand, as it were,
God in reaching down to man descends as far as the Divine Logos
and no further. The realm of the Divine Logos is in the *kosmos
noëtos*, the intelligible world of concepts. The Logos does not

enter into the sensible world; it is the Powers which reach down into it.

It is Philo's view, in common with a frequent motif in Jewish tradition, that Father Abraham was the first man to come to recognize the existence of God. The form in which this idea is expressed in *Concerning Abraham* is the following: Ur, the birthplace of Abraham (Gen. 11:27–32) was the center of astrology. Abraham found two deficits in astrology. One was that it supposed that the stars control the future; such a supposition ascribes to created things the power of the Creator, a view that is blasphemous to the point of being atheistic. The second deficit is that astrology depends on the sight of the eyes as they view the heavens; the senses, including sight, are fallible. A reliance on the senses is wrong in method and apt to lead to erroneous conclusions. Abraham's migration from Ur was his migration away from astrology with its two deficits; he moved away from the wrong method and the wrong conclusions of the astrologers. He came to Charran. Charran in Hebrew means "holes," "orifices," reminding one of the human body. Allegorically Charran means turning inward; that is, Abraham turned to a completely different method, the use of reason, and by it discovered that there was a logos, a capacity to reason, within himself. He then reasoned that by analogy there must be a Logos in the universe. By this new method, different from the faulty method of the astrologer, Abraham discovered the Divine Logos; this was equivalent to discovering the existence of God.

Reverting to Gen. 18:1, where Scripture states that Abraham saw and welcomed three visitors into his household, Philo assures us that the household was Abraham's inner being. God (in the form of Logos) enters into man's inner being, provided that man has arranged his inner spiritual household in the same orderly way that Gen. 18:2–3 tells us that Abraham arranged his physical household. The migration from Ur to Charran was one aspect of Abraham's progression by instruction. The orderly arrangement of his inner life illustrates another aspect of his progression by

learning. Again, Genesis, chapter 14, the war of the five kings of
Sodom against four kings of the East, represents the inner warfare between the higher mind on the one hand and, on the other,
the five senses and four passions, a warfare to determine which
would control, the higher mind or the senses and passions. Various other materials in the Scriptural account of Abraham are
similarly brought into relationship to progression by instruction.
The goal of an Abraham was to reach perfection, that is, to "see"
the Deity; Scripture tells that God appeared to Abraham (Gen.
12:1); in Greek "appeared" is the passive of the verb meaning
"to see" (as it is in Hebrew). That "God was seen by Abraham"
teaches that man can and should indeed make preparations to
receive the divine vision, but whether a man receives it depends
on God's grace.

In a long section (167–207), Philo deals with Genesis, chapter
22, which relates that God bade Abraham to take Isaac to a
mountain (Moriah) and there to offer Isaac as a sacrifice. At the
crucial moment, God through an angel intervened to prevent
Abraham from slaughtering Isaac. The allegory of the chapter
transforms it into the willingness of the progressing mind to sacrifice its joy (Isaac), but God does not wish man to make such a
sacrifice.[50]

We need to notice the comments that Philo makes in connection with Genesis, chapter 22. He says that certain quarrelsome
critics "who misconstrue everything" question what great thing
Abraham is supposed to have done, in the light of other instances
of fathers sacrificing their sons. Philo says that in these other
instances some motive existed, such as that of winning a war, or
else the offerer of the sacrifice wanted public acclaim. In the case
of Abraham, no such motive existed, for there was no war being
waged, and Abraham did the deed in the wilderness[51] so that there
was no possibility for observance and public acclaim. Presently he
turns to attack the captious critics: "Let them, therefore, set bolt
and bar to their unbridled evil-speaking mouths, control their

envies and hatred of excellence and not mar the virtues of men who have lived a good life. . . ." (167–207).

In a summary (273–276), Philo writes that God marvelled at Abraham's faith. He no longer talked with him as God with man but as "a friend with a familiar. . . ."[52] The crowning praise of Abraham is found in Gen. 26:5,[53] " 'This man did the divine law and divine commands.' He did them, taught not by written words but unwritten nature. . . . Such was the life of the first, the founder of the nation, one who obeyed the law, some will say, but rather, as our discourse has shown, himself a law and an unwritten statute."

While *On Abraham* provides major aspects of Philo's view of Abraham, there is infinitely more told about him in *The Allegory*.[54] There, far more explicitly than here, is Philo's use of Abraham as illustrative of the progress that you and I can potentially make, and which Philo feels that he himself has made; to this we will return (see pp. 85–86).

4. *On Joseph.* While Philo is extraordinarily (though not perfectly) consistent in his presentation, that is distinctly not the case with his treatment of Joseph. In *The Allegory*, Joseph is quite a negative character, symbolizing the politician, with all the pejorative overtones of the word as we use it today. Indeed in *On Dreams* II, 104 ff., Philo seems to treat Joseph as if he were a contemporary, a disloyal Jew like his own nephew Tiberius Alexander; such a person advances in power through the cheapest machinations and intrigues. In *The Exposition*, however, Joseph is the statesman, and thereby exactly the opposite of the politician.

Philo introduces the treatise by allusions to his previous essays on the lives of the patriarchs. The fathers were characterized by lives of instruction, self-teaching, and practice, but there is "a fourth life, that of the statesman," the description of which the treatise seems to promise to carry out. As scholars have noted, *On Joseph* does so only partially. For the most part the treatise is only a retelling of the biblical account, with the usual Philonic embellishments. The profundity which marks *On Abraham* is so noticeably missing from *On Joseph* that some scholars have questioned, gratuitously, whether it really belongs in *The Exposition*. Some have thought it an early essay from a time before Philo had fully developed his manner. Perhaps a better explanation is that the essay comes from Philo's old age, and reflects fatigue and a lack of zest.

In Philo's allegory of the figure of Joseph,[55] he makes a contrast between "polity," that is, the human governing of a city or state, and the Unwritten Law of Nature. The world, being a single Megalopolis (an idea expressed in *On the Creation*, and mentioned above, p. 54), is governed by the Unwritten Law of Nature; the city-states, unlimited in number, are diverse in politics and laws, this because of mutual distrusts and other deficiencies. They presumptuously "give the name of laws to whatever approves itself as advantageous." In Philo's total context, this disparagement of the laws of the city-states is useful in order for him to laud the Laws of Moses as superior to them.

The statesman is never the source of laws but only an administrator of them. *On Joseph* depicts the true statesman as immune to threats from popularity on the part of the mob. Moreover, he possesses self-control, especially in regard to women who cause great governmental upheavals—probably an allusion to the elopement of Helen with Paris and the ensuing Trojan War (54–56).

Philo's prolixity at its worst is manifest in a section respecting the effort of Potiphar's wife to seduce Joseph (Gen. 39:7–12). In the biblical account, Joseph, on the woman's first approach to him, spoke to her of his unwillingness to betray the trust of his master and to sin against God; she kept approaching him, and, as a climax, caught him by his coat, saying "Come lie with me." Joseph promptly left the coat in her hands, fleeing without saying a word. In Philo's account, Joseph's speech to her takes place while she is holding the coat (42–48); Philo says that "he [Joseph] spoke long and wisely." In Scripture, the wife grabs him by the coat at a time when none of the men of the house were indoors; as Philo writes about this, the house could scarcely have remained empty of men for the duration of the long oration. It is possibly right that Joseph spoke wisely, but if so, one must say that his words in Philo are remarkably stuffy.

Deficient as *On Joseph* may be as a totality, possibly it was incumbent on Philo to write the treatise because of the role of Joseph in Scripture. One moves on from *On Joseph* to *On the Life of Moses* (which we saw above), and from there to the treatises *On the Decalogue* and *On the Special Laws*.

5. *On the Decalogue.* This treatise has a structure similar to that of *On Abraham*, that of a balance between piety, man's relation to God, and the cardinal virtues, man's relation to men. The first five commandments reflect piety, the second five the cardinal virtues. But since the cardinal virtues are almost everywhere regarded as numbering four, Philo encounters an arithmetical difficulty, for he must make the last five commandments fit in with four virtues. He is, of course, quite able to overcome this difficulty. He does so by regarding "Honor your father and mother" as intermediate between piety respecting God and the virtues respecting men.

The essay has a certain eloquence,[56] despite its wordiness. In Philo's context, he has moved from creation, through the patriarchs as exemplars of the Unwritten Law of Nature (and the treatises *On Joseph* and *On the Life of Moses*); he will go on after this treatise to the four treatises *On the Special Laws*. *On the Decalogue* presents main "headings" or "topics"—Philo speaks of them as "summaries"; the ensuing four treatises *On the Special Laws* will present in detail what *On the Decalogue* presents as the major topics.[57]

Philo does not enumerate the Ten Commandments in the way that the modern synagogue does, nor does he follow the same sequence.[58]

It was noted earlier (p. 48) that the Sinai episode is absent from *On Moses* I, though it appears in *On Moses* II. *On the Decalogue* deals in detail with aspects of the Sinai episode, namely, the Ten Commandments there revealed. Yet Philo completely abstains in this treatise from mentioning Mount Sinai; rather, he concentrates his attention on the Wilderness as the place of the revelation, as if the sacred mountain did not exist. He tells that Moses promulgated his Laws in the depth of the desert instead of in the cities because "most cities are full of countless evils, both acts of impiety toward God and wrongdoing between man and man." He proceeds to defend the views that "the Laws were not the inventions of a man but quite clearly the oracles of God." Some of these God delivered in his own person, and some through his prophet Moses. The "headings" or "summaries" of *On the Decalogue* God "gave in his own person and by his own mouth alone"; the particular Laws, presented in the four books *On the Special Laws*, were spoken through the prophet Moses.

There is a sense in which Philo on the surface seems to be involved in a contradiction in connection with the particular Laws. Their literal divine origin as revealed through the prophet Moses is explicit. But, on the other hand, the particular Laws, being only copies or imitations of the Unwritten Law, are, at least externally, in the same category with the laws of the city-states. The superiority of the Mosaic Laws over the laws of the city-states is twofold: one, the Mosaic Laws are everywhere the same, but the laws change if one moves from Athens to Sparta to Alexandria; two, the Mosaic Laws are eternal and unchangeable, whereas in some city-states a new king can abolish inherited laws or introduce new ones, and therefore the laws of the city-states are neither eternal nor unchangeable. The implicit contradiction lies in Philo's assertion, on the one hand, of the divine origin of the

Mosaic Laws and, on the other hand, his apparent assigning them to the same category with the laws of the city-states in that they are only imitations of the Unwritten Law. But this is only an apparent contradiction; it is a by-product of Philo's utilizing the categories of Stoic distinctions between the Unwritten Law of Nature and the particular laws.

6. *On the Special Laws.* Philo treats these in four books. Book One, though it touches on the existence of God and man's inability to know God's essence, and on proselytes and apostates, is primarily concerned with worship: the Temple, the priests and Levites, the high priest, and the sacrificial system, as these are presented in Scripture. Philo attacks the Greek mystery religions (319), admonishing that no followers of disciples of Moses "either confer or receive initiation" into such rites.

Philo's manner here is to present the biblical materials, first with philosophical embellishment, and then by allegorizing the Laws. He does the same in the other three Books.

Book Two deals first with the matters of the oath, based on not taking the name of the Lord in vain (1–38). Next, he explains the Sabbath, the New Moon, and the other sacred days of the calendar (39–222). Next comes the application in particular ways of "Honor your father and mother" (223–241). The book closes with the punishments for disobedience of the first five commandments (242–256), and with the assertion that the rewards for obedience are virtue as its own reward.[59]

Book Three deals first with marital chastity and prohibitions of sexual aberrations based on "Thou shalt not commit adultery" (7:82). Next (83–168) come the subjects of murder and homicide, including a section on the "Cities of Refuge" for the latter (Num. 35:11–12; Deut. 4:41–43). Philo turns next to the biblical laws on assaults that fall short of killing (169–204), and then reverts to murder and to defilement through contact with a corpse.

At the beginning of Book Three, there occurs one of the rare instances in his writings wherein Philo speaks of himself (1–6). There had been a time, so he writes, when he had had leisure for philosophy and for contemplation of the universe and was exempted from "base and abject thoughts" and did not grovel "in search of reputation or of wealth or bodily comforts." He was able to bless his lot in having escaped from "the plagues of mortal life." He was now, however, plunged into "the ocean of civil cases."[60] If unexpectedly there is some lull in the civil turmoils, he has been able to turn back to his contemplation. Yet he must thank God that, though submerged in these cares, he was not sucked down into the depths but retained the ability "not only to read the sacred messages of Moses but also to . . . unfold and reveal what is not known to the multitude."

Book Four deals with the last three of the Ten Commandments, "Thou shalt not steal"; "Thou shalt not bear false witness"; "Thou shalt not covet." In connection with the first of these, Philo cites biblical laws, particularly those against burglary, kidnapping, and the loss through theft of something deposited. He treats too of theft which leads to worse crimes, including perjury.

Under false witness, Philo discusses subservience to the mob, the deceits of practisers of divination, and the obligations of judges. Under covetousness he speaks of the need to regulate the desire for food, this through the dietary laws, explaining the latter in some detail.

He then proceeds to relate the particular Laws to the virtues; again, though only passingly, he sets in balance piety on the one hand and the cardinal virtues on the other. But as he does not wish to repeat himself, so he says, he proceeds with only a mention of piety in relation to the virtue of justice. Under this topic he discusses kingship, that is, the obligations of the ruler. He moves on to discuss the general rules of justice, such as honesty in commerce, biblical laws against ploughing with an ox and an ass together, or wearing a garment woven of two materials (Lev.

19:19; Deut. 22:10–11). He then deals with warfare, citing the biblical laws respecting terms of peace, consideration of the women of the vanquished (Deut. 20:10–18), and the prohibition of destroying fruit trees (Deut. 20:19–20). He ends with praise of justice as the offspring of "equality," viewing equality as so inherent in nature as to be manifest in the order of the universe, exemplified by sun and moon and the seasons of the year.

7. *On the Virtues*. Following as it does on *The Special Laws*, this treatise is a logical sequel, since Philo has consistently equated scriptural laws and the virtues. But why has Philo included within *On the Special Laws*, Book Four, the section noted just above on justice? Would not this section logically have been the initial part of *On the Virtues?*[61] Has some scribal caprice or an accident resulted in disarray? Furthermore, one could have expected to find in *On the Virtues* the usual balance that Philo presents between piety on the one hand and the four cardinal virtues on the other hand, but if a section on piety was ever part of *On the Virtues* (as some think), then it has disappeared. Scholars who have inquired into these problems have not found in the surviving manuscripts[62] of Philo's writings any clue to a solution. But perhaps the explanation is that Philo was guilty of not providing what scholars have unreasonably expected: pure consistency.

*On the Virtues* has some other surprises: Philo does not adhere to the usual listing of the cardinal virtues, which are justice, prudence, courage, and temperance. Rather, the component parts of the treatise are given under the following sub-headings: On Courage (1–50); On Philanthropy—also called On Humanity[63] (51–174); On Repentance (175–186) and On Nobility (187–227). This deviation from the expected seems to be of no great significance, for these sub-topics deal with man's relationship to his fellowman. Moreover, within On Courage and On Philanthropy, Philo provides material on Moses (such as his choice of

Joshua as a successor) which reasonably could have been part of *On Moses* but was not presented there. If we ask why Philo proceeds as he does, we find no ready answer.

On Courage first exalts that virtue in peacetime, illustrated in the inner courage of the sick or the poor who ignore material disabilities. Philo then treats of courage in wartime, drawing on material found primarily in Deuteronomy, chapter 20 (on exemptions from military service), and Num. 25:1–18 and 31:1–18 (relating to the foe, the Midianites and Moabites).[64]

Philo begins his sub-section, On Philanthropy, with the statement that humanity is the virtue closest to piety and is its sister, and even its twin. Yet he does not develop this theme; instead, as if he has lost the train of his thought, he reverts to the greatness of Moses, exemplified in his not conveying his authority as successors on his own sons. Moses knew and admired his lieutenant Joshua; he did not immediately designate Joshua, but rather prayed to God that he choose the successor. Once Joshua was so designated, Moses was filled with intense joy and was not depressed by his approaching death.

Philo then paraphrases the poems in Deuteronomy chapters 32–33. The body of Moses, he says, then began to be stripped away and his soul to be laid bare as it yearned for its removal from the body. Moses alone "had grasped the thought that the whole nation from the very first was akin to things divine"; this kinship to the divine was a "far more genuine tie than blood." What Moses possessed, he gave his people ready for their use; what he did not possess, he prayed that God grant to them. The fountains of the grace of God, though perennial, are not "free for all, but only to suppliants. And suppliants are all those who love a virtuous life. . . ."

Philo goes to present some of "the ordinances which he [Moses] gave to posterity": the prohibition against taking interest from a fellow-Jew; the prohibition against withholding a hired man's pay even overnight; the principle of allowing the poor to "glean" in the fields and vineyards; and other laws (51–101).

He then speaks of proselytes (102–104) and of immigrant so-journers who are not proselytes. He summarizes a variety of laws (106–174), many of which he had treated in *On the Special Laws*.

The sub-section, On Repentance, is very brief (175–184). Repentance as a virtue is second to piety, having the same relationship that recovery from illness has to good health. Absolute sinlessness belongs to God alone, or possibly to a divine man. When Moses convokes repentant people so as to initiate them into his mysteries, he invites them with conciliatory and amicable offers of instruction. Repentance is appropriate not only respecting delusions, such as revering created things rather than God, but it also can be the passing from mob rule into democracy.[65]

The sub-section, On Nobility, contends that the truly well-born person is the wise man, the ignoble is the fool. The possession of gifted or of virtuous ancestors is of no benefit to their descendants unless they inherit the gifts or follow the virtues. For example, Adam was born nobly, but sired Cain; Noah sired Ham. Adam was moulded in body by God, and received his soul from the breath of God; "his father was no mortal but the eternal God." Yet Adam chose the base and the evil, with the natural consequence that he exchanged immortality for mortality.[66]

Examples are found too in Jewish history. Abraham had many children, but only one [Isaac] "was appointed to inherit the patrimony. All the rest failed to show sound judgment and . . . were denied any part in the grandeur of their noble birth."[67] So, too, with Isaac and his sons, ignoble Esau and noble Jacob (unnamed in the text).

On the other hand, there are those whose ancestors were men of guilt but who in their own lives were worthy of emulation. "The most ancient member of the Jewish nation was a Chaldaean by birth, the son of an astrologer." (Philo does not give Abraham's name here.[68]) Abraham "is the standard of nobility for all proselytes."[69]

A second example is Tamar[70] (Genesis, chapter 38). Bred in polytheism, "she deserted to the camp of piety. . . ." The handmaidens of Leah and Rachel, Bilhah and Zilpah (all here unnamed), rose to virtual equality with their mistresses.

Enemies of the Jews and of mankind assume as their own precious possession the nobility which does not belong to them. There is no doctrine more mischievous than to hold "that avenging justice will not follow the children of good parents if they turn to wickedness, and that honor will not be the reward of the good children of the wicked." The Law assesses each person on his own merits.

8. *On Rewards and Punishments.* Because this treatise in part repeats material found especially in *On Abraham* and *On Moses*, possibly it should not be classified within *The Exposition.* It seems to be an independent essay, a summary prepared in Philo's old age, possibly after the pogroms of A.D. 38.

A sub-title is often printed in editions of Philo which is in reality supplied by a passage in Eusebius (*Ecclesiastical History* II, 18:5). In that passage, the treatise is spoken of as dealing with "rewards and punishments *and curses.*" Rewards and punishments are dealt with in 1–78. Next comes a section (79–126) which some scholars treat as an independent writing, and call it On Benedictions. The next section (127–161) is also at times regarded as independent and is known as On Curses.

Assuming that the treatise as a unit—which seems unlikely—Philo reverts to the three-fold plan of Moses in his writing of the Pentateuch (found in *On Moses* II, 46 ff.): Creation, the historical material, and the legislative material. He then repeats here what he has presented on Enos, Enoch, and Noah in *On Abraham.* His treatment of Noah is both briefer than that in *On Abraham* and, moreover, Philo tells us that the man "in whose day the great deluge took place is called by the Greeks Deucalion and by the Hebrews Noah."[71]

He turns next to the three patriarchs, the triad "holier and dearer to God," belonging to one family, a father, a son, and a grandson. He describes Abraham, though without mentioning his name, ascribing his achievement of perfection to instruction; but here Philo's emphasis is on the faith of the patriarch (Gen. 15:6). Isaac, mentioned by name, gained his virtue through nature and without a struggle; Jacob, by contrast, gained his through practice, "by means of constant striving." He attained to the vision of God, which showed him "that He is," but "not what He is . . . God alone is permitted to apprehend God." Philo goes on to say that some "distinctly deny" that God exists; "others hesitate and fluctuate"; "others whose notions . . . are derived through habit rather than thinking . . . believe themselves to have successfully attained to religion, yet have left on it the imprint of superstition." The best class are those "who have had the strength through knowledge to envisage the Maker and Ruler." As we saw above (pp. 59–60), there are those who through the senses, rather than through reason, apprehend God; such persons constitute Israel ("God seer"), the people who see that God exists. The name Israel is "ill-sounding"[72] but excellent in its meaning; Philo here has in mind the ordinary, non-intellectual Jew. He speaks of the reward each of the patriarchs received in attaining to the divine vision. He then comments on the transition from the active life of youth to the gratifying contemplative life of old age.

As to Moses, he possessed piety in a special degree; Philo here alludes to what he has written in *On Moses*, repeating the fourfold offices (king, legislator, prophet, and high priest), but now he calls them rewards.

He proceeds to speak of the rewards bestowed on the houses and families descended from the patriarchs, aligning their individual gifts with the characteristics of the patriarchs, instruction, intuition, and practice: "From this household, increased in the course of time to a great multitude, were founded flourishing and orderly cities, schools of wisdom, justice, and holiness: where the rest of virtue, and the acquisition of it, is the sublime subject of inquiry" (1–66).

Philo now turns from rewards to punishment. He gives as the first example Cain, who, rather than being slain, was punished by living forever in a state of dying. He next mentions Korah (though not by name) and his associates (Numbers, chapter 16).

It is at this point (#79) that some editors of Philo,[73] as we have said, insert a title, "On Benedictions." Philo paraphrases biblical passages[74] which speak of blessings; indeed, he hopes that "when the wild beasts within are fully tamed, the animals too will become tame and gentle. . . ." Another blessing will be wealth in the sense of plenty of good (Lev. 25:3–5; Deut. 11:13–14; 28:6). There will ensue the blessing of healthiness in the body (Deut. 7:15).

On Curses begins at #127. The first curse is poverty, through the loss of crops, followed by the sterility of the earth. Thereafter comes slavery, and then diseases of the body (Deut. 28:22–35; Lev. 26:16). By contrast with such misfortunes on evil Jews, proselytes will be exalted by their happy lot (152). Again by contrast he speaks of the blessings of the neglected sabbatical years, for the land, after a rest, will produce an improved class of people.

The curses and penalties just described fall on those "who disregard the holy laws of justice and piety, who have been seduced by the polytheistic creeds which finally lead to atheism, and have forgotten the teaching of their kin and their fathers." If such people accept punishments as a warning and then repent, even if they are enslaved, they will one day experience liberty (Deut. 30:3–5). Then those now scattered throughout the Greek world will arise and hasten "from every side with one impulse to the one appointed place [the Temple in Jerusalem], guided in their pilgrimage by a vision, divine and superhuman, unseen by others but manifest to them as they pass from exile to their home" (165). They have their three intercessors: first, God's clemency and kindness; second, the holiness of the ancestors who, their souls released from their bodies, do not cease "to make supplications for their sons and daughters," since their prayers are heard; third, their spiritual reformation. At that reversal, the enemies "who have mocked at their lamentations, proclaimed public holidays on the days of their misfortunes,[75] feasted on their mourning . . . will . . . find that their misconduct was directed not against the obscure and unmeritable, but against men of high lineage."

Whether *On the Virtues* and *On Rewards and Punishments* are properly to be classed within *The Exposition* is contestable, as we have seen. Yet these two treatises fit more congruently with *The Exposition* than they do with the other categories of Philo's writings.

A treatise, *On Providence,* has as a totality survived only in Armenian. Fragments of it have survived in Eusebius; these fragments are from what seem to be the second of two parts of the treatise. A Latin translation of the Armenian was published by J. B. Aucher in 1822, along with a Latin translation also from the Armenian of *On Animals.*

In form, *On Providence* is a dialogue between Philo and a doubter, Alexander. Perhaps this Alexander is Philo's apostate nephew Tiberius Alexander. The first fragment (in Eusebius, *Preparation for the Gospel* VII.21) is very brief; it is a defense of the view that the doctrine of providence is not refuted if one believes that a certain amount of matter, enough for the universe, was on hand for God at creation.

The second fragment (*Preparation for the Gospel* VII.14) begins with Alexander's contention that the wicked prosper and the good do not, and hence there is no providence. Philo's reply is that punishment is often only deferred, not nullified. Moreover, the prosperous wicked are not truly happy, nor are their physical acquisitions of any value to God or to the wise. As to certain instances which Alexander had cited, Philo insists that ultimately they were punished, if only by mental sufferings.

Alexander has also raised the issue by the citing of disasters such as storms and earthquakes and ravages by savage beasts. Philo gives his refutation—without ever citing Scripture. Indeed, the only Jewish item in the surviving fragment is Philo's allusion in #64 to his having been in Ascalon in the Holy Land "on my way to the ancestral temple to offer up prayers and sacrifices."

While *On the Eternity of the World* is customarily printed in the collections of the writings of Philo and is often ascribed to him, only a minority of scholars regard it as authentically his. The principal basis for denying the work to Philo runs as follows. In many of his writings, Philo has dealt with God's creation of the world. God is omnipotent over the universe, even to the point of being able to destroy it, should he wish. However, if the world is destructible, it cannot be eternal; to believe in the eternity of the world, then, is in effect to deny God's ultimate power over it. Precisely because the treatise affirms the eternity of the world, the majority of scholars deny the treatise to Philo. However, Colson (Loeb Classical Library IX, p. 173) believes that in the essay Philo is not speaking for himself, but a bit too vigorously quoting other people; hence Colson thinks that the denial of Philo's authorship is extreme. All in all, though, the treatise, genuine or not, is relatively unimportant.

## C. The Allegory of the Law

*The Allegory of the Law* is a long series of treatises, each of which, as we have said, begins with a scriptural passage. The following are the treatises in this category and the biblical passages utilized at the beginning:

| Latin Title | Translation | Biblical Basis |
|---|---|---|
| *Legum Allegoriae* I | *Allegories of the Law* | Gen. 2:1–3, 5–14 |
| " " II | " " " " | Gen. 2:18–3:1 |
| " " III | " " " " | Gen. 3:8–19 |
| *De Cherubim* | *On the Cherubim* | Gen. 3:24; 4:1 |
| *De Sacrificiis Abelis et Caini* | *On the Sacrifices of Abel and Cain* | Gen. 4:2–4 |
| *Quod Deterius Potiori Insidiari Soleat* | *That the Worst Is Wont To Attack the Better* | Gen. 4:8 |
| *De Posteritate Caini* | *On the Posterity of Cain* | Gen. 4:16 |
| *De Gigantibus* | *On the Giants* | Gen. 6:1–4 |
| *Quod Deus Immutabilis Sit* | *On the Unchangeableness of God* | Gen. 6:4–12 |
| *De Agricultura* | *On Farming* | Gen. 9:20–21 |
| *De Plantatione*\* | *On Planting* | Gen. 9:20 |
| *De Ebrietate* | *On Drunkenness* | Gen. 9:20–29 |
| *De Sobrietate* | *On Sobriety* | Gen. 9:24–27 |
| *De Confusione Linguarum* | *On the Confusion of Tongues* | Gen. 9:1–9 |
| *De Migratione Abrahami* | *On the Migration of Abraham* | Gen. 12:1–3 |
| *Quis Rerum Divinarum Heres Sit* | *Who Is the Heir of Divine Things* | Gen. 15:2–18 |
| *De Congressu Quaerendae Eruditionis Gratia* | *On Mating for the Purpose of Education* | Gen. 16:1–6 |
| *De Fuga et Inventione* | *On Flight and Finding* | Gen. 16:9, 11–12 |
| *De Mutatione Nominum* | *On the Change of Names* | Gen. 17:1–5, 15–22 |
| *De Somiis* I\*\* | *On Dreams* | Gen. 27:12–15 |
| " " II | *On Dreams* | Gen. 37:7–10 |

\* This book is often regarded as Book II of *On Farming*.

\*\* A lost treatise also on dreams preceded this treatise; we inherit the second and third of three.

Brief summaries of the treatises in *The Allegory*, such as given above for *The Exposition*, are not readily feasible. This is the case because the treatises in *The Allegory* are kaleidoscopic or even "stream of consciousness" in manner. The words, phrases, and sentences of Scripture lead Philo into such digressions that there is seldom a discernible clear thread of exposition. These treatises are hard to read simply because of the absence of a connected thread. This is especially the case when Philo weaves into his exposition new citations of passages from Scripture and turns to expound these, however far afield doing so may take him. An honest reader can find his attention flagging and, in all candor, boredom can begin to set in. This is all the more to be pitied in that the content of *The Allegory* is at least as important as that of *The Exposition*, and contains the fullest exposition of Philo's essential thought and character. Students have found it helpful in counteracting the possible tedium to begin to read with an interest in some particular topic, whether justice, the mystic vision, the role of Sarah, or the virtues, and to read with the intent to discover what Philo says on the particular topic. It is also helpful in reading the treatises to use the Indexes referred to above (p. 22). The use of these Indexes can alter what is unclear into something clearer or even reasonably clear, when Philo, seemingly in an abrupt way, introduces a biblical character.

In between the prolix and admittedly dull passages, there are other passages which are quite exciting and of such insight as to repay the time and attention required for the reading.

The reading should alert the reader to the wide range of Philo's philosophical ideas, and to the difficulties involved in arranging them into some orderly system. Philo never undertook this chore. Systematic exposition has been undertaken in German[76] and French[77] and, happily, also in English.[78] If one can legitimately distinguish between philosophical ideas on the one hand, and motifs that are of concern in the discipline called "the history of religions," the index in Erwin R. Goodenough, *By Light, Light: the Mystic Gospel of Hellenistic Judaism*, can often be useful in guiding a student to such ideas.

## D. Questions and Answers to Genesis and Exodus

*Questions and Answers to Genesis and Exodus.* These writings have been preserved consecutively only in an Armenian translation.[79] In 1826, J. B. Aucher published a Latin translation of the Armenian; the C. D. Yonge[80] translation renders Aucher's Latin. For the Loeb Classics in two volumes, Ralph Marcus used the original Armenian, not the Latin translations. Fragments in Greek of these books have been periodically discovered and published.[81] Apparently the material on Genesis in the original Greek was divided into six books, but the Armenian into only four. That on Exodus, in two books, begins with Exodus, chapter 12, and runs through 28:34. That is to say, neither Genesis nor Exodus are completely covered; Genesis, chapters 1, 11–14, 21–22, and 29–50, do not appear at all. Nothing is preserved respecting Leviticus, Numbers, and Deuteronomy, probably because Philo never got to them.

All the treatises in *The Allegory* are on Genesis; there are overlaps in content between *Questions and Answers to Genesis* and *The Allegory* when the same biblical content is used. Philo's ordinary manner in *Questions and Answers* is to ask why the biblical verse says what it does, or else, what is the meaning of the verse as he quotes it. Almost invariably his answer respecting the literal is very brief, and he gives an elaborate philosophical explanation, and frequently proceeds to an allegorical interpretation. Since there is so much overlap in content between *Questions and Answers to Genesis* and *The Allegory,* scholars have wondered why the two presentations. My published suggestion that *Questions and Answers* is mostly on the order of preliminary notes for treatises, some of which Philo wrote and others he planned but did not get around to, has met with approval by those who have seen it.[82] Where there is no overlap with *The Al-*

*legory*, we are provided with additional materials which fill out the details of Philo's allegorical interpretation, and hence this material is of considerable consequence. Ralph Marcus closes his translation in the supplementary volumes to the Loeb Classics translation with an English index to *Questions and Answers*.

The student should avoid reading Philo in the Yonge translation. It is ponderous and heavy, and often inaccurate. The Loeb Classics edition is the one which readers in English should use. For the beginner, some of the notes on the Greek text in the Loeb Classical Library will be of little utility; the explanatory notes, on the other hand, are very helpful.

I have at times advised students to be prepared to be unable to absorb the sense of some passages, whether in *The Allegory* or in *Questions and Answers*. Let the student record these passages and move on; later, after more absorption of the totality of Philo, let him revert to those passages, for their sense may become clear after further reading. Let the student remember that Philo's message is relatively simple: train yourself to rise up into the intelligible world, the world of concepts. Simple as this message is, it could not be presented with greater complexity than Philo manages to achieve.

If in part the complexity can be ascribed to Philo's verbosity, to his piling up of synonyms and synonymous phrases, there is still another explanation. Philo is an expounder of Scripture, and whatever Scripture chances to present, he feels duty-bound to explain. If Scripture repeats, Philo feels called on to justify the repetition, usually by discovering a distinction that implies that the two passages are not truly repeating. If Scripture chances to utilize some seemingly awkward expression, Philo seems to feel he is forced to explain it. Conversely, in the course of his making a philosophical point, he recalls a Scriptural passage that seems to him relevant.

The complexity in Philo, then, arises primarily as the direct result of his effort to explain Scripture philosophically. This complexity characterizes *The Allegory* and *Questions and Answers*, rather than the historical writings and the Exposition.

Can the treatises not related to events, such as *Against Flaccus* and *Legation*, be dated either absolutely or relatively, whether they are early in his career or late? The effort has been made, but not persuasively.

# 4

## Religion in Philo

This chapter repeats some of the material covered in the résumés of Philo's writings. But more significantly, the presentation will in some measure reappear in Chapters 5 and 6. Why do I provide two basic presentations? Simply because the two presentations are necessary for a balanced understanding of Philo's thought. Obviously, Philo's religion was Judaism and is therefore centered in Scripture; the first presentation is essentially biblical, the second philosophical topics.

Philo presupposes the validity of the doctrines and the demands which Scripture presents, such as laws and sacred days to observe. Perhaps a better term for our purposes is Philo's religiosity, rather than Philo's religion. Religions as long-lasting as Judaism or Christianity produce the phenomena of diversity within a common tradition, as exemplified in the diversity between Roman Catholics and Protestants in a common Christianity, and, within Protestantism as between the elaborate ritual of the Episcopal Church and the ritual bareness of the Society of Friends. Such inner diversity has often been rooted in historical events or personalities, or in some concentration on or exaltation of a limited range of doctrines or practices. The distinctions between Roman Catholicism and Protestantism, basic as in some senses they are,[1] do not extend to the totality of Christian phenomena; Roman Catholics and Protestants have Scripture in common and observe sacred days such as Good Friday, Easter, and Christmas on the same days. By and large the keynote to the religiosity of a usual Protestant[2] communicant is his individualism and freedom. By religiosity one means the tone and character of the carrying out of the religion on the part of differing personalities within the tradition. Religiosity can and does vary, as between the cold rationalist and the emotional individual, or as between the communicant, zealous to fulfill all the obligations, and the communicant content with a bare minimum of fulfillment.

Philo's religiosity was quite unique and distinctly different from that presented and advocated in the Rabbinic Literature. To labor the point, his religion was not distinctly different from that of the Rabbis,[3] but his religiosity was. One clue to the distinction in religiosity is the place of the Laws of Moses. In Rabbinic Judaism the Laws are an end in themselves; in Philo they are a means to what he conceives of as a greater end. There is no echo I know of in Rabbinic literature of the central goal in Philo's Judaism, that of mystic communion with the Godhead.

As repeatedly hinted at in reviewing Philo's writings, Scripture was for him not only the recording of ancient events but also the contemporary experience of everyman. Without allegory, Scripture as contemporary experience might have been difficult or even impossible; the use of allegory made it readily possible. Genesis, accordingly, is both the experience of its cast of characters who lived long ago and the experience of you and me today.

At creation, the first man (Gen. 1:27) was the Platonic idea of a man. The first man, being an idea, never came down to earth, and never had any material existence. On the other hand, God fashioned Adam (Gen. 2:7) out of dust of the earth, and he breathed spirit into him. The earthly Adam, then, was a mixture of the material body and of the immaterial soul. So are we. Our bodies pull us towards what is material, what is evil. Our souls pull us towards what is immaterial, to what is good. When we are born and while we remain babes, we are entirely subject to our passions, our bodies (symbolized by Egypt). When we grow older, we enter into the vice of adolescence (symbolized by Canaan). While traversing adolescence, we begin to become reasoning creatures.

Since man is capable of reason, Adam is allegorically the mind, a possession we all have. Eve is sense-perception; the mind functions first through the senses, and therefore mind and sense-perception needed to be joined together. Adam was a mind of ordinary quality, neither gifted nor deficient; minds vary among us in quality, but basic to all of us is the first task of the ordinary mind, to receive and sort out the perceptions by the senses.

Placed in the Garden of Eden, which allegorically is the idea of virtue, the serpent, allegorically "pleasure," intruded; when mind and the senses become bent on pleasure, they lose virtue through expulsion from its domain. "Adam" and "Eve" also lost the perceptible four cardinal virtues, represented in Scripture by the four rivers which flowed out of Eden (Gen. 2:10–14). We, too, if we succumb to pleasure, forfeit virtue.

Having lost virtue, Adam-man could have succumbed to despair. What distinguishes us from animals is our possession of hope, expressed in Scripture (Gen. 4:26) through Enos, who "hoped to call on the name of God."[4]

From hope we can move, along with the Scriptural narration, to the next stage, that of Enoch, repentance, the blotting out of our past trespasses. We can come next to the stage of Noah, tranquility. Tranquility is not our final destination, but only the last of the three preliminary way-stations, for Noah represents a "relative righteousness," as is clarified when Scripture (Gen. 6:9) speaks of him as "righteous *in his generation*."

When we achieve tranquility, we are ready for our major journey, which is along the royal road to the vision of God. Our ability to make that journey depends on our innate gifts. Some of us possess adequate gifts, some of us do not. For those of us who possess them, these gifts number three: the ability to learn, intuition, and progress through practice. These native gifts are presented in Scripture in Abraham, Isaac, and Jacob. The historical patriarchs each made the journey on the royal road and came to the divine vision by possessing all three gifts, yet in each of the patriarchs one of the three gifts dominated, and the dominating gift gives the clue to the character of each of them. Allegorically, the patriarchs represent the Graces, God's gifts to men. If we possess the gift of the capacity to be instructed, there is an Abraham in us; if we possess intuition, there is an Isaac in us; if we can practice, there is a Jacob in us.

How do these gifts work? They work in us as they did in the patriarchs. Let us take the Abraham gift as our chief example. He was born in Ur, the center of the error of astrology; all of us are born and reared in areas where error is omnipresent. Abraham's migration from error was a spiritual journey, one we too can make, for we can migrate spiritually from the error inherent in our environment as he did from his. We can abandon the reliance on our senses which is the wrong way of astrology and like astrology leads to wrong conclusions. We can, like Abraham at Charran, turn inward, turn to our reason, and we can also infer from the existence of a logos in ourselves that there is a Divine Logos in the universe.

As we move along and gain through being instructed, we can have our higher minds regiment and control our five senses and four passions (based on Genesis, chapter 14) and thereby establish democracy, inner harmony within us. We can furthermore traverse the Encyclical Studies (that is, we like Abraham can mate with Hagar, Genesis, chapter 16) as a preliminary to our mating with Sarah (who is true philosophy and also generic Virtue). If we create order in our inner being, as Abraham created order in his household (Genesis, chapter 18), God will come into our inner selves. Accordingly, if we can in these ways prepare ourselves, then God may, if He chooses, grant us the privilege of a vision of the divine (Gen. 12:1).

Just as we can live like Abraham, if only we have his gifts, so too we can live like Isaac or Jacob, if only we have theirs.

Isaac serves Philo in two ways. In one, Isaac is allegorically "joy," the spiritual joy that a man attains on his reaching perfection. In Philo's allegory, God, not Abraham, is the father of Isaac—joy—for no man begets his own happiness. Rather, joy is begotten by God out of virtue (Sarah), and virtue presents joy to the perfected man. In a second way, Isaac represents perfection achieved by intuition. Aristotle has supposed that the three ways of attaining perfection were by instruction, practice, and intuition; he had, however, doubted that perfection through intuition is really attainable. Philo nevertheless so describes Isaac. He also describes Isaac as "self-taught," apparently meaning this in contrast to Abraham who profited through instruction. Philo seems to regard Isaac as superior to Abraham in that Isaac was born perfect, but Abraham needed to progress in order to attain it. That Isaac should be ranked above Abraham is surprising; probably this arises strictly in allegorical terms, and Philo does not mean that the historical Isaac was superior to the historical Abraham. Rather, Isaac is Philo's way of illuminating perfection through intuition.

As to Jacob, his perfection was attained through practice. That is, the virtuous things that Jacob did brought him to the spiritual goal. In his treatment of Scriptural passages about Jacob, Philo stresses deed rather than inner thought, his usual way with Abraham. The literal text of Scripture, as will be recalled, portrays Jacob as doing some things of dubious ethical import to Esau. Just as the Rabbinic sages so reinterpreted the passages so as to have Jacob emerge as a righteous man and Esau unrighteous, so too Philo retells matters to vindicate the patriarch. The progression through deeds led Jacob ultimately to his wrestling with the evil inherent in his innate being and overcoming it (Gen. 32:

24–32). Thereby the final alteration takes place, for Jacob becomes changed into Israel. Israel, as we have said, means "he who sees God." That is to say, Jacob achieves the goal of spiritual perfection to the point of symbolizing the essence of Judaism, the collective Israel who rise to the vision of God.

That is, we in our spiritual journeys can be like the patriarchs, if only we have the superlative gifts with which they were endowed.

The three patriarchs lived before Moses and his promulgation of his Laws. In order for us to live like the patriarchs, we need to possess *orthos logos*, that is, impeccably correct reason. All gifted humans, if they have the requisite personal gifts, and practice *orthos logos*, whether they are Jews or Gentiles, can live like the patriarchs and rise to the same vision of God that the patriarchs achieved. All such people are citizens of the megalopolis, the "great city," and they live by "nature," within the intelligible world. Such people can become members of God's family, and become prophets through whom God speaks to mankind. Indeed, they go on to achieve spiritual joy which virtue bears to them, as the virgin Sarah bore Isaac to Abraham, with God being the "father" of this joy.

But suppose we lack the great gifts of the patriarchs, are we doomed? Not at all. The patriarchs were incarnations of the Unwritten Law of Nature. When we escape from our enslavement in Egypt, our individual enslavement to our bodies, we pass through the Wilderness. The Wilderness purifies us from the vices that gripped us in the cities of Egypt, for the city is inevitably the place of vice. We are led, as Israel was, to the mountain which is the high point of the Wilderness, the place where each of us may experience God as did the Hebrews in the time of Moses. Thereafter, the Laws and the rituals all fit into place in our making order in our individual lives. The legislation which begins in Exodus, chapter 20, as simply a recording of the deeds of the patriarchs, means that if we obey the Mosaic Laws, we will be living like the patriarchs. There are those among us who will so live without full awareness that they are doing so; these literalists conform with the "lower mystery."[5] But those of us who know the allegorical meanings and live by the Laws with full awareness of their relationship to the patriarchs, conform with the "higher mystery." A Jew is a man of Israel, and Israel is "the race" which sees God. Even those Jews who lack the exceptional gifts of the patriarchs can live in the intelligible world of spirit and immortality.

What the above means is that Philo, who himself "sees" God, considers the journey to the divine vision as the goal of his Judaism. His use of philosophy is directed to explaining the nature of God, of the universe, and of man, so that men, understanding these things, can attain the goal. In this sense, the philosophy in Philo is subordinate to the religiosity. Philo explains not for the sake of explaining, but in order to encourage men to move onward to the mystic goal of Philo's own personal mysticism.

The Bible, especially the Pentateuch, is both the account of the ancient patriarchs and also the guide for our own spiritual progression. The Bible is thus contemporaneous with us, for it speaks of our own experiences. We, as it were, relive the ancient experiences in our own lives.

If by chance we are perplexed, or insecure, or faulty in our understanding of ourselves, recourse to the Bible will remove our perplexity, our insecurity, and any faults in our understanding. The Bible gives us secure assurance, for it carries us along, protecting us in our growth from babyhood through adolescence and its distractions into the safety of mature spiritual achievement. The Bible is the vehicle for bringing us into communion with God. Such communion is the purpose and indeed the essence of religion. All else, including the Mosaic Laws, is secondary. The Bible is the vehicle; man rides forward by means of that vehicle.

# 5

# God and Man

We turn now from following the sequence of the biblical narrations to presenting the basic ideas in Philo's philosophy in the form of topics, never forgetting that for Philo the function of the philosophy is to enable man to understand his spiritual adventure. In presenting these facets of Philo's philosophy, we bring together matters which are ordinarily not brought together by him, but are presented in random ways in his various writings. Philo, unhappily, abstains from providing his system; there is a risk that is necessary to run in our making his system possibly too neat.

The clues to understanding Philo's conceptions respecting God are the following. 1) Passages in Scripture provide explicit statements, many of which Philo regards as axiomatic. Other passages provide only implicit notions, some of which Philo blends with the explicit. Still other passages prompt him to interpretations, often against the letter of Scripture, but necessary for some consistency on his part. 2) Philo's explanations of the nature of God are primarily Platonic. What in Scripture is axiomatic achieves justifying explanation by recourse to philosophy. Conversely, there are to be found philosophical statements that are buttressed or even justified by the citation of scriptural passages. 3) Much of what Philo says about God has to do not with what God is, but with what men can come to know about God. Since men vary from each other in their native gifts, God is to be understood by men in terms of the variations in human capacities. A man who is both bright and educated will understand God in a way different from a dull and uneducated man. 4) In modern theological analysis, especially respecting the Hebrew Bible, it is customary to use two terms: *transcendent* is used for those views of God that so exalt Him as to suggest that He is above and beyond this world; *immanent* is used for those passages that suggest that God is in close relationship to or even direct contact with this world. Whenever within a religious tradition of some long duration there occurs an emphasis on God as transcendent, there arises an accompanying need for man to bridge the gap between him and the transcendent God, for the reason that if God is conceived of as outside the world, man is in effect left without God. In the Old Testament, angels, messengers who have been sent by the transcendent God to man or who carry man's appeals up to God, bridge this gap. Angels, as it were, are the device by which the transcendent God becomes immanent.

Two somewhat different impulses are often involved in a religion in the development of views of God as a transcendent Being. One of these impulses seeks to protect God from what is seemingly trivial, or seemingly unbecoming to him. For example, can God be the source of evil in this world? If the answer is given as no, then how can the presence of evil be explained without reducing in any way God's unique sovereignty? This can perhaps be done by ascribing the source of evil to some underlying force, such as Satan in the prose prologue to Job, or by ascribing evil to certain angels subservient to God. That is, God has often been conceived of as transcendent so as to shield him, as it were, from seeming to possess traits that are not admirable. A second impulse in the development of views of God as transcendent arises from what we might call ordinary human experience. For example, an avalanche coming down a mountainside seems to be headed towards a village below, but then turns away and the village is spared. No one in the village has received a communication from God about the avalanche, and no one has seen God in the act of turning it aside. Did God directly save the village? Or was there something in the contours of the land as he had shaped it that diverted the avalanche? The point here is that men do not ordinarily encounter God himself in the events of their ordinary days. The world seems to operate as if God is not involved in it. In olden days, that is, in the time of Abraham or Moses, God was directly an actor in daily events in that he spoke in understandable speech and, from time to time, acted; in our time he neither speaks articulately to any of us, or appears visibly to intervene in our affairs. In the sense that he is not visibly or tangibly involved in our lives, he is transcendent. If we believe that God turned the avalanche aside, that conclusion does not rest on our having seen him do so, but in our reasoning that he must have done so. If we can see him and hear him, we are spared the need to reason about him; we are impelled to reason about him simply because he is not visibly and tangibly involved in our affairs. When we have recourse to our reason in connection with God, inevitably we conceive of him as transcendent.

For Philo, God is transcendent. Since Scripture presupposes that God exists, his existence is an axiom for Philo. We can know that God exists, but as to our knowing *what* he is, Philo repeatedly assures us that we can never know that. Our reason, acute and penetrating as it may be, can never take us to the point of discovering what God is.

Philo's usual term for God as the transcendent, unknowable deity, is the Platonic term *To On*, "that which exists"; at times he uses another Platonic phrase, *To ōntōs On*, "that which *existingly* (that is, "truly") exists."

The biblical words *Theos* ("God") and *Kyrios* ("Lord") are distinct in meaning from *To On*. Not to notice and understand that they are distinct can mean missing a keystone in Philo's philosophy. In Philo's view the two biblical terms *Theos* and *Kyrios* have to do not with the essence of God (which is unknowable), but with activities, past or present, on his part that are knowable. The activities of God are knowable, even though God himself is not. *Theos* alludes to God's activity in that he created the world; *kyrios* alludes to God's on-going activity in governing the world. God in his essence, indeed in his fullness, is much more than the creator and the ruler. His having created the world and his on-going rule of it are knowable facets of the Unknowable God. The term which Philo uses for the divine activities, past or on-going, is "powers" (in Greek, *dynameis*). We might here define a power as a single facet of a multi-faceted *To On*. There are, of course, more powers than the two of past creation and on-going rule.

Since we men live in this world, we can know through our experience that the world exists. However dull we may be, we are able to reason from the fact that creation has taken place that there was a Creator behind the creation. Again, if we are somewhat brighter, we can observe the regularities in the universe; the sun rises in the East and sets in the West, and summer follows spring and autumn summer. We can therefore reason that the universe is ruled, and, accordingly, that one facet of God is his rulership of the world. Yet respecting God's creation and rulership, we men begin with what we observe in this world; that is, we reason from what our senses have perceived. The Powers reach down from the transcendant *To On* and act immanently in this sensible world and our senses here encounter creation and rule. Our senses provide the raw materials for use by our minds.

Philo has called where we live the "world of perceptions" or else "the sensible world." If I see or feel a tree, I am in the sensible world. If out of seeing or feeling many trees I move on to fashion an idea about what trees are, I have moved into the world

of concepts, into the intelligible world. I make this move by utilizing my reason.

But the domain of *To On* is not only beyond our senses, it is
even beyond and outside our reason.

God is nameless;[1] he is spoken of in Scripture as God of Abraham, Isaac, and Jacob, solely for the purpose of enabling men to
address prayers to him. When a man speaks of his characteristics,
that is, his "attributes," such a man is in effect trying to define
what by axiom is not definable. The root meaning of define is to
limit. When one tries to define God, one is at the same time lim-
iting him. By axiom, God cannot be limited; hence, God cannot
be defined. To speak of God as good, or holy, or just, is to define
him. Philo assures us that to apply such attributes to God is totally impossible. The "attributes" can be expressed only in the
negative; that is, one can say, "God is not unjust," but not "God
is just." Statements about him are simply efforts on the part of
men to speak the unspeakable; in this sense one may liken him to
roles known to men by such terms as Craftsman, Parent, Father,
Cause, Planter.[2] But these terms do not describe him totally, and
hence they do not really describe him at all.

In between the distant and remote domain of *To On* and our
sensible world there lies the world of concepts, the intelligible
world. The sensible world is the one in which our senses operate;
the intelligible world is the one into which reason enters when
once it has left the senses behind it. At times we come into the
intelligible world by having risen above the sensible world; at
times we are in the intelligible world by inferences that our reason makes from the domain of *To On*.

Inasmuch as *To On* is in essence unknowable, especially to the
senses, Scriptural statements about God, whether they are explicit
or implicit, are usually treated by Philo as being within the intelligible world. In the case of the Powers of creation and rulership, though they indeed belong to the intelligible world, they
reach down immanently into the sensible world. That is, the

three domains, that of *To On*, that of the intelligible world, and that of the sensible world, are interconnected.

Whatever we can know or say about God, whether through what Scripture tells us, or through our reason, belongs within the intelligible world. It is not only the Powers that belong there, but there too is located the Divine Logos, Divine Reason. The multifaceted capacities of God, which we can know through our reason, are summarizable in the Divine Logos.

At no time does Philo, in the abundance of what he has to say about the Logos, ever define Logos for us. What we can do here is assemble some of what Philo tells us, and out of that material hope to present some sense of what Philo intends by the term. We can begin with two balancing statements. One, since God as *To On* is unknowable, Logos is the knowable aspect of God, because *To On* reaches down into the intelligible world in the form of the Logos. Two, since *To On* is by definition beyond man's capacity, man, in striving to reach God, can go as far as the Logos and no further. Logos, then, is the intersection in the intelligible world of *To On* and man, as God reaches down to man and as man reaches up to God. Logos can be explained as the substance of what we can know about God and about his functions. Accordingly, whatever Scripture tells us that God or the Lord said or did, Philo ordinarily ascribes to the Logos.

The utility of Logos to Philo is that it is his major means of solving the paradox of transcendence and immanence. Thus, on the one hand, God is complete in himself, self-contained. He is "The Place," containing himself within himself spatially.[3] That man cannot grasp the essence of God means that Philo can say that God is the prime Good, but he is beyond Good in whatever way our limited capacities enable us to conceive of goodness.[4] In effect, the uniqueness of God is so absolute that the inference could be drawn that God is shut off from the world. It is an axiom in Philo that matter is evil; he is unwilling to bring God into direct contact with matter. On the other hand, Logos is the device by which God can be affirmatively viewed as connected with the world. The actual divine contact with the world accordingly is ascribed to the Logos.

The Logos never descends from the intelligible world into the sensible world; man must move into the intelligible world to encounter the Logos. As we have said, when Abraham was still in astrology, using the sense of sight as his eyes kept ranging the heavens, he was still in the sensible world. That changed when he went from Ur to Charran; there Abraham abandoned the reliance on his senses, turning instead to reason. In having done this, he discovered the capacity to reason (logos) in himself, and concluded by analogy that there must be a Divine Logos in the universe. It was in this way that Abraham came to the recognition of the existence of God and thereby departed from astrology which, relying on sight, was a wrong method that led to wrong results. The Divine Logos is God's Reason.

Figures of speech may be helpful. We might say that the Logos is an offshoot of God, but a phrase of this kind does not appear in Philo. The phrase that the Logos is the son of God, with wisdom as the Mother, does appear, this in connection with Philo's identifying the high priest with the Logos; indeed, Philo speaks of the Logos as God's "first-born son" (*Agr.* 31) or oldest son (*Conf.* 146–147).

Other things that Philo tells us about the Logos are superficially fraught with inconsistencies. The Logos on the one hand is the totality of all the "ideas" which reside in the intelligible world; on the other hand, the Logos is the single supreme "idea," from which all other archetypal ideas emanate. Allegorically, Moses is the *hieros logos*, a phrase difficult to render in English, though the idea is not. *Hieros* can mean sacred, or it can mean priestly. *Hieros logos* would mean "sacred reason." Inasmuch as Scripture, of which Moses was the author, has provided mankind with the guidance for living, which is completely rational, Scripture is the sacred, priestly rational Logos. (The student should be alerted to the circumstance that in the Loeb Classics edition, the Greek text in alluding to Scripture reads that the *hieros logos* has taught x or y; the translation there reads, rather, that Moses taught this x or y.)

Respecting Moses as the embodiment of reason, there is an additional complexity to consider, that of the distinction common among the Stoics between thought and speech.[5] When thought is fully reasonable, it can be called logos. But since we can often fail to say in words precisely what we are thinking, speech in a sense distorts our thought. Unuttered thought is capable of being pure logos, but speech impairs the purity of thought. When Philo speaks of Scripture as *hieros logos*, he means that Scripture, properly understood, is the purity of thought which is also Moses. Scripture as utterance is speech, that is, the mere letter of Scripture, represented allegorically as Aaron.[6] He who has been inducted into the processes of allegory can move from the "speech" of Aaron, that is, the literal sense of Scripture, into the "thought" of Moses, who is the Logos.

As to the allegorical identification of the high priest with the Logos, the intent is to imply that the observances of the Jewish cult ceremonials (which observances are in the sensible world) represent something higher which is in the intelligible. Hence, Philo allegorizes the Passover as the passing of the soul out of domination by the body, and explains the abstinence from pork, the sweetest of all meats, as the practice of self-control. But the basic idea must not be lost sight of: the cult observances are the medium by which the loyal and observant Jew can be united with the Divine Logos.

Moreover, since, as we have said, the Logos is the totality of archetypal ideas, Logos as "reason" has some synonyms; for example, virtue, wisdom (in Greek, *sophia*), and pure philosophy. Sarah is one of several biblical characters who in Philo's allegory represents virtue, or wisdom, or true philosophy.[7] Abraham ultimately attains to Sarah; also, Gen. 26:5 which tells that Abraham did[8] all of God's law means that Abraham "did" the Divine Logos, for the Divine Logos is the Law.[9] Thus, Abraham "does" virtue, wisdom, and true philosophy.

Since the Logos, to repeat, is the totality of archetypal ideas, it follows that there are many *logoi* (plural of logos) within the Logos. Professor Wolfson, in dealing with Philo's world of ideas, contends that Philo differs from his mentor Plato in that the latter considered the ideas as eternal and uncreated,[10] whereas Philo viewed them as created by God. In some senses Logos and the totality of the ideas are one and the same. Ideas, in Plato's view, are not passive; they not only are causes but also possess active power, being able to spur or stimulate imitations in the sensible world.[11] Conversely, every "imitation" in the sensible world necessarily has a balancing idea in the intelligible world. Philo appears to regard ideas-powers as classifiable into categories, which for our purposes we may regard as four. One category is that of beneficence, and includes goodness, mercy, concern, grace, and creativity. A second category is that of authority, including rulership, legislative power, regal power, and even the power of punishment. A third is the *logos tomeus*, "cutting[12] reason," cutting in the sense of making valid distinctions as opposed to lumping together matters which differ from each other. A fourth—though some analysts might prefer it as within the second category—is the *logos spermatikos*, "seed-bearing reason," which prompts or spurs a man to some novel or fresh insight; since such insights can be plural, one should speak of *logoi spermatikoi* in the plural.

To repeat, at times in Philo's presentation the entire intelligible word is contained within the Logos, but at times the Logos is viewed as distinct from the other aspects of the intelligible world.

Two principal questions arise about the Logos. One is somewhat difficult to formulate, but possibly it may take the following form: Does Philo regard the Logos as a reality, as a distinct entity having real existence, or is the Logos no more than an abstract construct, convenient to Philo's philosophy, but without true existence? Scholars have espoused both views, for the reason that there is no decisive clarity in Philo's presentation.

The second question may throw some light on the first: What is the background of Philo's Logos theory? Obviously it has some Greek ancestry, for at the least the word, and some aspects of the idea, are known to be even earlier than Plato. The term is especially prominent, however, in Stoic thought, serving there as the reason which is in-dwelling in the universe and thereby available to all thinking men. One would, of course, never use the adjective "divine" in connection with the Stoic logos. There is also a Jewish ancestry to logos, found in the idea of wisdom. A passage, 1 Kgs. 3:5–12, tells that Solomon prayed to God for gifts, and inasmuch as he did not pray for long life or wealth but only for wisdom, God granted him wisdom. That is to say, wisdom is a gift from God. Various passages in Scripture, such as Job, chapter 28, describe how impossible it is for men to acquire wisdom by their own efforts, but it can be acquired only as God's gift. So fully associated is wisdom with God that it was present at creation and available to him as he fashioned the world (Prov. 8:22–32). That God bestows it makes wisdom kindred to God's revelation, and in a sense *Torah*, "divine teaching," and *ḥokma*, "wisdom," are synonymous. The presence in Scripture of the Book of Proverbs, a book of wisdom, by its mere presence, alters wisdom, that is, true wisdom, from a human attribute into a divine capacity which rare men come to possess. Moreover, there are passages in Proverbs, such as chapter 8, wherein wisdom is personified; she builds a house, she beckons to people.

When Greek and Jewish thought met, after the conquest by Alexander the Great in 323, the inter-penetration of ideas brought it about that Hebrew *ḥokma* was equated with the Greek *sophia*, and *sophia* with both Torah and Logos. There took place, before

Philo's time, a Hellenistic Jewish amalgam in which Torah-logos were already intertwined with each other. Such an amalgam is found in the Wisdom of Solomon.

It is not unreasonable, then, to ascribe both Greek and Jewish ancestry to Philo's Logos theory. That there exists a Logos is part of Philo's Jewish heritage; the various explanations of how Logos operates in the intelligible world is essentially his Grecian culture.

It was said above that, in Philo's view, ideas had a certain power, and *logoi spermatikoi* could reach down into the world of men and spur them to reason. But a reverse process is also possible, whereby man reaches up into the intelligible world. The connection, whether from the intelligible world down to man or from man up into the intelligible world, is through man's higher mind. The mind of man is double. The lower mind is that which receives the perceptions of the senses, sorts them out, and even responds to them. (In medieval philosophy the lower mind is often known as the "animal" mind. A dog sees a bone; the dog's mind receives the perception. It thereupon directs the dog to walk to the bone.) The higher mind draws concepts out of the perceptions received by the lower mind. The higher mind cannot function without the lower, nor the lower without the senses, but the higher mind has no direct connection with the senses. Indeed, the higher mind can be higher only as it frees itself, or is set free, from the errors that are inherent in the senses and in the lower mind.

Philo uses an abundance of synonyms for the higher mind: *nous*, *dianoia*, *logismos*, and even logos. In part the higher mind seems to be a thing, in part it seems to be a process or an activity.

The higher mind is the antithesis of the senses which are functions of the body. The passions, which can distort man's thinking, are also in the body. That is, the higher mind is the antithesis of body, for the higher mind is altogether immaterial, and the body is material.

Hence, whatever else in man is immaterial is in a sense synonymous with the higher mind, for example, the soul (*psyche*). So synonymous do higher mind and soul seem to be that a distinction between them is elusive. Perhaps the following may suggest the distinction: the soul is the seat of man's awareness and consciousness, and it encompasses not only the higher mind but also the conscience. The soul even includes the *elenchos*, "discipliner"; the *elenchos*[13] is the inner restrainer which, consistent with the demands of conscience, warns or restrains the soul from capitulating the demands of the body. The soul, then, is the totality of that aspect of man which is immaterial, while the higher mind is that portion of the soul wherein the capacity to reason dwells.

When man's soul, or man's higher mind, is freed from the impediments of the body, as we have said, man can rise into the intelligible world. In such freedom from the body, men passingly move into "immortality"; when literal death takes place, it is only the body which dies, while the soul takes its place permanently in the intelligible world of immortality. If it is asked, precisely where in the intelligible world does the immortal soul go, Philo confesses to uncertainty. Perhaps the soul is resorbed into the universal soul; perhaps it enters a star.

Soul/higher mind are man's means of entrance into the intelligible world. Within the sensible world, the senses exist, which Philo grades in descending order: sight, hearing, smell, taste, touch. The passions, which number four, lust, greed, hunger, and anger, make demands for the satisfaction of bodily desires and needs. Capitulation to the passions and the senses leads to evil action; resistance to them leads to virtuous action.

It is Philo's assumption that the higher mind of the gifted man is capable of countering the bodily demands; it is capable of choice, being able to elect to counter the bodily demands or to succumb to them. The poorer the quality of a man's mind, the less apt it is to elect to counter the demands; the better the quality, the more apt it is to do so.

In a general sense, Philo believes in free will. Also, in a general sense, he rejects the notion of fate which, strictly speaking, is exactly the opposite in implication. Fate is related in a way to divine providence in that both seem to negate free will. But fate is an impersonal force and is "inexorable"; that is, fate cannot be prayed to with the end in view of altering what is destined. Providence, on the other hand, in ascribing to God the control of human destiny, can be prayed to. Not being an impersonal force, God is subject to apparent alteration, should he will to alter something which he has earlier destined. Providence may limit free will, but providence does not necessarily negate it, as does "fate."

Since man, under God's providence, possesses free will, he is able to choose whether his higher mind will control his senses and passions or not. Man, if he is a Jew, can choose whether or not to observe the Law. Similarly, man can choose whether or not to prepare himself to receive the vision of God.

The goal of "religion" is to rise above corporeality and to achieve this vision of God.

# 6

## Political Theory

What are the components of a properly governed society? In Philo's overall view of Scripture in *The Exposition*, as we have seen, he began with creation, then moved on to the "general" laws, next treated of the statesman, thereafter presented an account of Moses and the four offices he held, and finally moved on to the "special" laws. Especially in *On Moses* II, and very frequently in *The Allegory*, he deals with the components of the well-governed society: the king, the elders, and the population. The Jews, in his view, comprise a *politeuma*, which we might translate as a "political" entity. In part, Jews dwelled in the Dispersion, among non-Jews; in part, Jews dwelled in Judea where Gentiles in some abundance were to be found. Accordingly, Philo's thought about Jews as a *politeuma* required him to distinguish among a host population, and transient or permanent outsiders.

Two curious factors of omission are to be noted. One is the almost complete silence of Philo about the state of affairs in Judea in his lifetime, in that he abstains from mentioning the Maccabean dynasty which had reigned from 150 B.C. to the Roman conquest in Judea in 63 B.C. The reign of Herod the Great, 37–4 B.C. is likewise unmentioned. The three sons of Herod who inherited his client-kingship (Antipas, tetrarch of Galilee; Archelaus, "king" of Judea; and Philip, northeastern trans-Jordan) are never mentioned. As is well known, the Romans had deposed Archelaus in A.D. 6, and Judea was thereafter ruled by Roman procurators. One of these, Pontius Pilate, as we saw (p. 45), is mentioned; so too is Herod Agrippa I whose presence in Alexandria touched off the pogroms of A.D. 38. That is to say, in Philo's political theory, the role of the monarch in Judea in his own time and in the period immediately before him plays no role whatsoever.

Similarly, the second omission is striking, namely, the almost complete absence of any allusion to David as king or to his dynasty. David is mentioned as the psalmist, never as the king.[1]

The conclusion from these omissions is the following: Philo is concerned more with the situation of the Jewish community in Alexandria as part of a unique *politeuma* than with the Judean situation and experience. He expresses this concern in terms of an ideal "constitution." Within his statements about the ideal there enter allusions to situations regarding the Jews in relation to the Roman rule, but these allusions are somewhat peripheral to his espousal of Scripture as containing the perfect constitution. In his allusions to Roman rule, Philo had to be guarded in what he wrote, lest Romans learn of it and regard his views, as well as him, as subversive. We have already noted that in *The Allegory*, Joseph is treated not as the statesman he is in *The Exposition*, but as the cheap, opportunist politician; Joseph in *The Allegory* is recurrently a veiled description of a wicked Roman official. As to the Roman emperor, Philo so couches what he has to say that it is only by implication that he asperses Roman rule; that is, by describing the "constitution" of the Jews as ideal, Philo can imply the shortcomings of Roman rule and imperial pretensions without specifically saying so. Yet, although Philo presents the ideal constitution as derived from Scripture, the substance of his presentation is Grecian, owing a debt to Plato, Aristotle, and the Stoics.[2]

As to the king, there appear to be two facets to his presentation. One facet we might call the theory of kingship, the other the application of that theory to Philo's view of the role of Moses and thereafter Joshua. Respecting theory, Philo's view of kingship conforms with Hellenistic thinking. The king, that is to say, the legitimate king, was the philosopher-king. He exceeded his fellow men in wisdom as well as in physical stature. The role of his wisdom was his ability to free his higher mind of the impediments of senses and passions, so that his higher mind could soar into the realms of the ether, there absorb the general law of nature, and thereafter transform these unwritten laws into written statutes consistent with the law of nature. What made a royal law legal was its promulgation by a philosopher-king. If by chance the king was a tyrant, or at the other extreme an incompetent weakling, then obviously he was not a philosopher-king, and his statutes were not consistent with the law of nature, and therefore not truly "legal." The philosopher-king could, by his higher mind, establish "democracy"; he did so in his personal inner being by regimenting his senses and passions so that all parts of his being were in perfect equilibrium. Having established "democracy" in his soul—democracy being the state of affairs in which the higher mind keeps all the parts in perfect equilibrium—he could similarly establish democracy in his kingdom. It is to be noted, of course, that this view of democracy, apparently Platonic in origin, is not what we today mean by the term; our American system could well have been scorned by Philo as reflecting what he despises as ochlocracy, "mob rule."

A philosopher-king, by having absorbed the law of nature, thereby himself becomes a *nomos empsychos koi logikos*, a law articulate in a man.[3] As we have seen, it is Philo's view that the patriarchs Abraham, Isaac, and Jacob were such men; so, too, in a supreme way, was Moses. Philo has a Scriptural basis for regarding at least Abraham as a king, this in the Septuagint rendering of Gen. 23:6, wherein the Hittites say to Abraham that he is "a king"[4] among them. Since Abraham was never a reigning king, we are here in the realm of Philo's theory, not actual history. The history enters in, however, in Philo's treatment of Moses, which we saw in the summary above (pp. 47–52) of his two-part treatises on Moses. There Philo had ascribed four roles to Moses: king, law-giver, priest, and prophet. There needs here to be added to that material certain statements which Philo makes, respecting how Moses came to be designated, and the matter of the succession to Moses by Joshua rather than Moses' children. As to the appointment of Moses, Philo is critical of certain pagan procedures wherein a king was designated by lot.[5] He seems to approve of the election of the king by the whole people.[6] but he scorns an election by the votes of men who are hirelings.[7] He, of course, scorns those who achieve kingship through the power of their military resources. When the populace elects a king, God himself adds to this favorable vote by setting his seal of ratification on the election. Philo also says that rulers are appointed by "nature,"[8] but nature and God are in this sense synonymous. Philo also says, respecting Moses, that he was appointed by God with the free consent of those whom Moses would govern, since God brought about a willingness of the people to make the voluntary choice.[9] Moses did not convey his authority to his children (as did pagan kings), but transmitted it to Joshua who was spiritually worthy.

The superiority of the king over his subjects, a basic assumption of Philo, requires him to express a significant reservation. Pagan kings had come to regard themselves as divine; Philo will not accept the literal divinity of a king. Yet Exod. 7:1 portrays God as saying to Moses, "Behold, I make you a God over Pharaoh." Philo says that while a king is the same as other men, in the power of his authority and in his rank, he is like God himself,[10] there being nothing on earth higher than he.[11] But Philo cannot ac-

quiesce in deifying a king, even a Moses, to the point of removing
him from the mortality of all men.

Scripture (Num. 11:16–17) speaks of a chosen group of seventy
elders who are to join with Moses in bearing his great burden.
Out of this passage there arose in Judea the later practice of a
Sanhedrin of seventy-one people who in Maccabean times and
until the destruction of the Temple constituted the legislative-
judicial governing body there.[12] In Alexandria there was a *gerousia*, a council of elders; it is assumed that such local councils
existed in other large Dispersion cities. Philo, as Professor Wolfson points out,[13] alludes a number of times to the seventy men
who advised Moses, but at no time does Philo bring this body
into relationship to his view of the Mosaic "constitution."

Rather, Philo deals instead with the corporate Jewish people.
Recalling now that Gentiles were to be found in Judea, and Dispersion Jews lived in a Gentile environment, Philo needs to distinguish among categories: those who by birth belong to the host
people, those who are temporary sojourners, and those who are
permanent residents. Among the permanent residents in the
Jewish polity are those who, through conversion of Judaism,
enter into it (as there are those who through apostasy leave it).

In addition to the term *politeuma*, Philo also speaks of Jews as
constituting an *ethnos* ("nation"), composed of the twelve tribes;
they are kinsmen and indeed brothers. All Jews are equal before
the law, except in the case of hereditary priests and bastards who
have a special higher or lower status. So much for "the native
born."

The body of sojourners includes proselytes. (Philo uses both
this term and the term *epelytes;* in etymology both words come
from the Greek word meaning "to come.") These proselytes
have come over to "the new and God-loving polity, and have
taken a journey to a better home, from idle fables to the clear
vision of truth."[14] While Philo notes Scriptural restrictions about

admitting Ammonites, Moabites, Edomites, and Egyptians (found in Deut. 23:4–9), he uses the Septuagint reading of Lev. 19:34 to conclude that proselytes possess equal rank with the native-born. He exhorts the host people, that is, his fellow-Jews, that such proselytes be treated both with respect and also with special friendship and more than ordinary goodwill. All members of the Jewish nation are to love proselytes as themselves, as friends and kinfolk in both body and soul.[15] Such equality and friendly treatment rests on Philo's conviction that the Jewish *politeuma* has as its basis not common ancestry but rather the spiritual import of the divine revelation.

And just as sojourners in Judea should be treated equitably,[16] so should Jews resident in Gentile lands. Such sojourning Jews have always paid some honor to their hosts, as in the prayers in the synagogues on behalf of the emperor.[17]

Philo seems also to envisage a class of individual Gentiles who, abstaining from entering the Jewish community, are proselytes in the sense of having abandoned polytheism, and have undergone, not a literal circumcision but a spiritual one, cutting off the pleasures of the senses and the passions. These "semi-proselytes" follow the law of nature—that is, they in effect conform to God, even though they have not entered into the Jewish ethnos.

Apostates are Jews who, in Philo's view, abandon their spiritual heritage and true religion and conform to the falsity and perversity of the Gentiles. There are passages in which Philo denounces certain people who asperse Scripture,[18] and it may well be that these are such apostates. Yet one must envisage what can possibly be called semi-apostates, those whose views or actions are subject to Philo's fault-finding, but who have not completely abandoned Judaism or the Jewish community. In *Mig.* 89–93 he speaks of "some who, regarding laws in their literal sense in the light of symbols of matters belonging to the intellect, are over-punctilious about the latter, while treating the former with easy-going neglect." Philo gently chides such people for allowing their allego-

rization of the laws to lead them to desist from the literal observance, and therefore Philo defends the importance of the literal,
and insists that these people should observe the laws: "Exactly as
we have to take thought for the body, because it is the abode of
the soul, so we must pay heed to the letter of the laws."

The extent of the semi- or full apostasy in Alexandria is unknown. Whether Philo's vexation about it implies an abundance
is not to be determined. But his vexation is clear.[19]

We move now, from king and people, to what Philo, and Josephus after him, called the Constitution, that is, the Laws of
Moses which begin in Exodus, chapter 20. It is the best of all con-
stitutions, even the ideal one. We must now take in account a
Philonic term we have already met: Megalopolis ("great city").
The term transcends its meaning. By megalopolis Philo means
the universe which God created. Just as every small city has its
constitution, so the universe possesses its. The constitution of the
megalopolis is the Unwritten Law of Nature and is in the intelligible world. The Mosaic laws, the Constitution of the Jews, are
the best possible approximation in the sensible world of the Law
of Nature, and are fully in conformity with nature.

The Constitution was promulgated in the depths of the Wilderness, not in the cities. (The cities are the locale for vice; the
Wilderness for virtue.[20]) The Laws had been promulgated under
circumstances by which the people could be convinced of their
divine character through miracles (described in Exodus, chapters
20–21). At that early time there was as yet no established society,
nor were there yet legislators who would have worked in accord
with some already-established form of government. Rather, the
Mosaic Laws were designed as the foundation for a society that
was to be formed in the future. Also, the journey through the
Wilderness had purified the people of the vice they had known
or even absorbed in the cities of Egypt. This unique assembly of

the Laws revealed through Moses was "a new constitution to be established by a new people in a new country" (Wolfson II, 381).

This Constitution, since it was for the megalopolis, was for all men, not for Jews alone. Or, to state this more precisely, Judaism was not for Jews alone; it was also for proselytes and semi-proselytes. Since Judaism was the sole true religion, it was necessarily applicable to all men. The Jewish *politeuma* was, to borrow a phrase, a body of true believers, transcending race and nation. But there were anti-Semites in the world, and there was a horrible pogrom in 38, and Jews were found throughout the Dispersion and were thus often aliens in alien lands.[21] What did the future hold for the Jewish people?

Philo saw a blessed future; he thought of a messianic age, even though he never speaks of a messiah or uses the term. He speaks of confidence in the future as assured by fulfillments in the past.[22] One such confident hope is the return of the dispersed to the Holy Land,[23] this based on Deut. 30:3–5. In the Holy Land there will be a rebuilding of the ruined cities, the desolate land will be inhabited, and a prosperity surpassing that of the past will take place.[24] Universal peace will come about, between men and men, and even between men and beasts.[25] And the foes of Israel will be punished.[26] A condition for such future bliss is repentance, coupled with divine mercy.

When that happy future comes about, so Philo believes, "each nation [will] abandon its peculiar ways, and, throwing overboard their ancestral customs, turn to honoring our laws alone."[27] That is to say, all nations, and the people that comprise them, will enter into the megalopolis, which is synonymous with Judaism.

The absence of a personal Messiah is the greatest distinction between Philo's messianic thought and the attendant range of views which became part of Rabbinic Judaism. There is no echo in Philo of the messiah as a son of David, of a great universal judgment day, or of resurrection. One might put it that Philo has a vision of a future messianic age, but completely without a messiah. The question cannot be answered whether his view was different from what became the view in Palestine because he did not know the Palestinian tradition, or that he knew, but rationalized and refined Palestinian views.

# 7

## Ethics: The Individual

Politics dealt in Chapter 6 with the corporate Israel. The concern in this chapter is the individual.

The suppositions in Scripture do not fully and clearly distinguish between man and the corporate body, since there the corporate community is usually viewed as the totality of individuals. Thus, the covenant in Scripture is expressed primarily in corporate terms in that its perpetuation was deemed dependent on the fidelity of the whole community to the Deity. If the community through its wickedness was untrue to the covenant, then the covenant was ruptured. In earlier prophetic thought, wickedness which could rupture the covenant was, for the most part, viewed as the consequence of an accumulation of evil over a period of time. While such accumulation was taking place, the Deity, by acts of punishment, was warning Israel that unless she mended her ways, the inevitable result would be that the evil had reached so high a point that the covenant was broken and God's protection forfeited. Yet within such Scriptural expressions relating to the corporate community, there arose a growing distinction between the righteous and the unrighteous, to the point that Ezekiel, chapters 18 and 32, set forth a full-fledged doctrine of individual-

ism, to the point of implying that the covenant had been transformed from being solely corporate into being supplemented by
application to each individual. Accordingly, while the fate of the
individual could be affected by God's protection of or punishing
anger at the corporate body, his individual destiny largely de-
pended on his personal righteousness or evil.

Especially in Deut. 30:15–20, it is set forth that the individual
man has the choice before him of life and the good, and death
and the evil, and man ought to choose the good. Reward and
punishment rested on the choice which the individual made. He
who was faithful to the revealed laws could expect the rewards
of prosperity, long life, an abundance of children. He who was
unfaithful underwent devastating punishment. So much, very
briefly, is the Scriptural pattern.[1]

How does Philo transform this basic pattern into his thought? In
answer, one needs to begin with an initial issue which can be
stated in the following way, that Scripture simply assumes that
man is free to choose evil or good. That such choice can involve
a complexity of moral dilemmas seems not to be raised in Scripture. Rather, it is held that man has in him both an impulse to
good and one to evil. The verse Gen. 8:21 reads as if the dominating impulse in man, arising at adolescence, is towards evil. But
in Scripture there is no extended development of the theme of
two impulses. Later Rabbinic thought spoke with some frequency
of both a good *yetzer* as well as an evil one,[2] but it does not probe
in any depth into the inner psyche of man. Rather, it concentrates
on deeds, not on what it is in man that prompts them.

Not only does Philo present such a probing with what is to be
described as some complexity, but his dualism of body and soul
is an important element in his probing. In a general way, it is his
view that those deeds which are associated with the body, especially with the gratification of the senses, are evil; those which
stem from the soul are good and are related to the virtues. The

worthy man seeks for the virtues, meaning in effect that man should live by the soul, this through rising above the body.

While there is an ultimate consistency in what Philo says about virtue and the virtues, he deals with these so frequently that variations in his presentation seem falsely fraught with inconsistency. For example, he speaks of "contemplative virtue" and "practical virtue."[3] He says of "contemplative virtue" that "it involves theory," for it is led into by philosophy, "and it involves conduct, for virtue is the art of the whole of life, and life includes all kinds of conduct. . . . The theory of virtue is perfect in beauty, and the practice and exercise of it a prize to be striven for."

But Philo also speaks of "generic virtue" as distinct from the four cardinal virtues, justice, prudence, bravery, and moderation. By generic virtue he means the idea of virtue in the intelligible world, contrasted with the four virtues that can be encountered in the sensible world, as exemplified in a man who is just or prudent. Respecting generic virtue, Philo uses a number of different Scriptural bases for illustrating it, through turning biblical matters into allegory. Thus, for example, the tree of life in Eden is generic virtue. So too is Eden itself. Again, Sarah is generic virtue, at least after her name is changed from Sarai.[4] When she was Sarai, she was "my sovereignty," that is, a particular cardinal virtue found in a man; when that man dies, that particular virtue also perishes;[5] it is generic virtue which is eternal, while the cardinal virtues are limited to the span of the life of the man who possesses one or more of the four.

Since the idea of virtue exists in the intelligible world, it must be untouched by anything material in the sensible world. Philo gives expression to this notion in his interpretation of Gen. 18:11, "it had ceased to be with Sarah after the manner of women," meaning that she had passed beyond menstruation. Philo interprets the verse to mean that Sarah was restored to virginity[6]—that is, the idea of virtue can have no contact with anything in the sensible world. In another passage,[7] he amplifies his explanation;

Sarah became generic virtue in that her passions were now calmed
within her. But in addition to Sarah's being allegorically generic,
archetypal virtue, she is also wisdom[8] and true philosophy.[9]
Hence, wisdom and generic virtue are synonymous. (Often by
"true philosophy" Philo means Judaism.)

Moreover, both in *On Abraham* and in *On the Decalogue* Philo
sets into balance piety (man's relation to God) and the sequel to
piety, namely, the four cardinal virtues. We need to recall the
relationship spoken of above, between *On the Decalogue* and the
four books *On the Special Laws;* we saw that *On the Decalogue*
contains what Philo calls "summaries," which we would call
"main topics," while *On the Special Laws* provided the details of
the particular laws associated with these main topics. In *On the
Decalogue,* the first five commandments are related to piety, the
second five to the cardinal virtues. *On the Special Laws* in effect
sets forth the specific requirements for living virtuously. If we
were momentarily to reverse the order of Philo's presentation, the
individual particular requirements are the "practical" virtues
which bring into the sensible world the intelligible idea of virtue,
with its synonyms of wisdom and piety.

The goal of righteous living is achieved when man, observing
the Laws of Moses, thereby progresses from this sensible world
into the intelligible world where virtue, piety, and wisdom abide.

The result of a man's reaching this goal is his attainment of
spiritual joy, allegorically represented by Isaac. Joy is the offspring of its mother virtue. Who is the father? God himself.
Philo's scriptural basis is LXX Gen. 21:1, which tells that God
"visited" Sarah; Philo adds "in her solitude." The imagery is
sexual: God is the father; however, the offspring that Sarah bears,
she bears not for God but for Abraham. That is, generic virtue
presents joy to him who attains to piety. So, too, in this same
passage, Leah, Rebecca, and Zipporah all become pregnant
"through no mortal agency."[10] (Lest we misunderstand, Philo
goes on to tell that God is the husband not of some virgin but

only of virginity!) Philo reverts several more times[11] to God as
the father of the joy which Sarah bears to the patriarch. The
account (Genesis, chapter 22) of Abraham's willingness to offer
Isaac as a sacrifice is allegorized to mean that the perfected sage
is ready to sacrifice his joy to God, but God does not wish such
a sacrifice.[12]

Philo warmly commends prayer in many passages. Never dis-
daining animal sacrifice, for it is prescribed in Leviticus, Philo
does not hesitate to commend prayer, if it is earnest, as a completely adequate way of worship. In two passages[13] he seems to
regard prayer as superior to sacrifice. Such sentiments, as is
known, are found in Ps. 51:19 and Mic. 6:6–8, and there is no reason for surprise at finding the same sentiments in Philo. Philo does
not demand the prayer be articulate; it can as worthily be silent.[14]

Commending repentance, Philo speaks about it relatively infrequently. As we saw above (pp. 69–70), a section of *On the Virtues* (175–186) deals with repentance. In the scale of values, the
primary place is held by healthy bodies, by ships that travel
safely, and by souls that never lapse into forgetfulness; "but
second to these stands rectification in its various forms, recovery
from disease, deliverance . . . from the dangers of the voyage,
and recollection supervening on forgetfulness. This last has for its
brother and close kinsman repentance. . . . Absolute sinfulness
belongs to God alone, or a godly man. . . ."

Professor Wolfson[15] presents a complex exposition of what
Philo means by virtue. He stresses correctly that virtue does not
mean the complete suppression of the emotions or passions, but a
control of them. Wolfson treats also of virtue as a golden mean.
But an easier definition of virtue than Wolfson gives is simply to
describe virtue as action consistent with the soul or the higher
mind, rather than the body.

Wolfson, moreover, ascribes to Philo a view different from
that of the Stoics, for whom virtue was its own reward. Wolfson

interprets Philo as meaning that virtues assume "a grander and loftier aspect" if, as recommended in Judaism, they are practiced for the sake of "honoring and pleasing God, that is, for the love of God."[16] I think that Wolfson is here mistaken, not in praising the honoring of God, but in so presenting matters as if the honoring or love of God is something other than or beyond the virtues. Philo writes that "those whose souls have ears" can hear God say: "My first rewards will be set apart for those who honor Me for Myself alone, the second to those who honor Me for their own sakes, either hoping to win blessings or expecting to obtain remission of punishments; . . . though their worship is for reward . . . yet . . . its range lies within the divine precincts." The Greek words which Wolfson translates "rewards," others translate "prizes." What Philo is saying—Wolfson to the contrary notwithstanding—is that the higher and lower motives, though different in gradation, are both in the realm of the virtues. I do not think that it is right to view the passage as dealing with reward for virtue; I think that Philo does not deviate from regarding virtue as its own reward.

Yet Scripture has many passages that promise reward for obedience to God's revealed will, and punishment for disobedience. Philo's recapitulation of these in *On Rewards and Punishments* is essentially corporate, though he makes some provision for individual reward, such as long life. But Philo is quick to add that the true long life is not measured in respect to a person's age but to his goodness.

What is strikingly absent from Philo is that aspect of reward and punishment in Palestinian thought wherein there is an afterlife to which rewards or punishments are deferred. Such deferral in Palestinian thought has as its motive the assurance that observable inequities in this life will be dealt with in the afterlife. Without the conviction that at some future time justice will ultimately be done, God can seem to be unjust. In Philo there is no hint of these matters, and no real concept of a future heaven or hell.[17]

Respecting afterlife, Philo has a doctrine of immortality, but it can be described as vague and pallid. As in the birth of an individual, body and soul-spirit become united, so at death they become separated, with the soul-spirit surviving. But what happens to the surviving soul? One recalls that soul can equal mind; it is man's higher mind that survives, while the lower, being associated with the bodily senses, perishes. The surviving soul, says Philo, "returns to the megalopolis . . . from which it originally migrated into the body."[18] Philo has based his views on LXX Gen. 15:15: "But thou shalt go to thy fathers, nourished with peace, in a goodly old age." Some people, so Philo says, interpret "fathers" to be referring to the sun, moon, and the stars.[19] Others think "fathers" is the intelligible world of ideas; still others regard "fathers" as the four elements, earth, water, air, and fire; but Philo adds that possibly the soul returns to the "fifth" element, the ether. What this latter seems to mean is the Stoic view of a universal soul from which the individual soul came, and into which it is to be resorbed.

But Philo seems to lean to another view, namely, that "fathers" refers to the "incorporeal substances and inhabiters of the divine world, whom in other passages [Moses] is accustomed to call angels."[20] In another passage,[21] Philo tells that at death Abraham became "equal to the angels."

If the domain of the angels, or of "the ether," means heaven, this is the nearest that Philo approaches to viewing the destiny of the righteous individual as being heaven. Perhaps in his environment there existed vivid views of heaven and its blessedness, or of hell and its tortures, but his rationalism would have impeded his espousal of such views. In Philo, immortality does not seem to be a reward for virtue. Rather, immortality is the ordinary sequel to a man's rising above his body; at death, his soul simply becomes separated from it. Immortality in Philo seems never to be conceived of as a reward, but only as a natural destiny.

# 8

## Philo's Achievement and His Character

In this chapter we draw together some threads of matters already presented. As we have seen, it is a commonplace in scholarly discussions of Philo to ascribe to him the first major reconciliation of Jewish revelation and Greek rationalist philosophy, such as were to become frequent in medieval Jewish and Christian scholasticism. There is no reason to challenge this assessment, but there is reason to inquire into it so as to isolate precisely what it was that Philo accomplished. It should be plain by now that we deal in Philo with matters beyond surface Hellenization, which means only the use of Greek words or Greek language. If we speak of reconciliation, then we mean a harmonization of elements that are basically different. On the first level, the obvious import of such a reconciliation in Philo was his utilization of the terms, phrases, and categories of Greek thought to explain and justify the claims and contentions of Judaism. But there is a more profound aspect. To understand it, we must recall that the concerns of philosophy and religion are largely the same. These concerns deal with the ultimate in man's situation, touching what he needs to understand and what his conduct at his best should be. Respecting conduct, whether in personal ethics or the role of human government, philosophy suggests what the conduct of man and men should be while religion prescribes it.

By the time that Greeks and Jews encountered each other in the fourth pre-Christian century, both civilizations had already created a body of written and oral materials related to these matters. By Philo's time, three hundred years later, there was even more material at hand in the two diverse legacies. The encounter had led into some comparison and some blending. A pattern of procedure in this blending, found in Fourth Maccabees, may illustrate aspects of this. It is there contended that he who possesses piety (this is a Jewish concept) thereby possesses the four cardinal virtues which the Stoics had taught: justice, righteousness, prudence, and bravery. Whereas ordinarily the Jewish documents relating to wisdom had focused on who is a just man or a righteous man (that is, they present concrete matters), the Greek documents focused on abstractions. These abstractions, when Jews learned them, served them as categories for explaining and justifying the concrete facets of Judaism. Involved in this level of blending is an aggregate of items which we can label as secondary.

There is, however, a primary matter which greatly exceeds the secondary in both importance and profundity: The Jewish ethics rested on the premise that God had revealed them to Moses and his successors; the Greek ethics arose out of a rational inquiry into the bases of the universe, with the end in view of defining its physical nature, of delineating the nature of man, and then of providing a rational explanation of what man's conduct should and could be. Jews, in a word, cherished their norms on the basis that God had revealed them, while Greeks propounded theirs on the basis that man's logical reason had disclosed them.

We have had frequent occasion to use and define the phrase, "the Unwritten Law of Nature." That phrase occurs very often in Philo; indeed, it is very basic to his thought. The phrase is older than Philo, but it appears only infrequently in the Greek

philosophical literature before his time. Helmut Koester, in studying the phrase, emphasizes that "for the first time in Greek literature the term 'law of nature' is liberally employed in the writings
of Philo of Alexandria." The key words here are "liberally employed";[1] there are at least thirty occurrences of the phrase in
Philo, plus additional synonymous expressions. Koester expresses
the opinion that "it is not possible to posit a Greek background
for Philo's [particular] use of the term," though the term, as distinct from Philo's special use of it is, of course, Greek. Koester
continues: "It seems more advisable to understand this term as a
fruit of Philo's efforts to unite basic elements of Jewish tradition
with the inheritance of Greek thought."

Before Philo, and even before Plato, two terms, *physis* ("nature") and *nomos* ("law") designated two different realms of experience. *Nomos* exists in the world of men and reflects the human effort to find some order in human "activities, customs, and
morality." *Physis*, on the other hand, is an orderliness, rational
and reasonable, but is not a function of human activity; rather,
*physis* is a realm of *nomos* which we might say is above man. In
one sense, *nomos* is an imitation in the realm of man of what is in
the realm above him, and, as a direct imitation, is thereby an extension of *physis*.

But in another sense *nomos* is not an extension, but rather the
very opposite of *physis*. To understand this latter we need to
hearken back to Greek dualism and to facets of Platonic and
Stoic thought, wherein "reality" lies in the realm of "ideas,"
while what is in the realm of humans is an imitation of or substitute for the idea. To use an example, a table made of wood is
"unreal," in that it can be chopped to pieces or burnt up; the
wooden table is an imitation of the idea of a table within the mind
of a carpenter, and that idea is not subject to be chopped to pieces
or burnt up, and is therefore "real." Everything in the human,
sensible realm is an imitation of or substitute for, an intelligible
idea. *Nomos* in the sense of an extension is an imitation of or sub-

stitution for *physis;* in the sense that *nomos* is kindred to a wooden table, it is the opposite of *physis. Nomos* is "unreal," *physis* is "real."

Greek Jews had given to the Pentateuch the title "The Nomos." Philo, as a legatee of Greek philosophy, needed to deal with both *physis* and *nomos.* Genesis, with its narratives and the absence of laws, belonged in "The Nomos" as the book of the "nomos physeos," "the nomos of nature." That is, *physis* and *nomos* in a sense become blended. The commandments which begin in Exodus, chapter 20, are the *nomos* of Moses, and that *nomos,* in the sensible world, is the imitation of the "law of nature." To repeat what we have already said, the pre-Mosaic patriarchs lived by *physis;* Moses later on in his laws recorded what it was that the patriarchs had done. In a sense, again to repeat, the *nomos* of Moses is an extension into the human realm of *physis* which operates in the higher realm; in another sense, *nomos* is the opposite of *physis* and inferior to it.

In relegating the literal *nomos* of Moses to an imitation of or substitute for *physis,* Philo seems on the verge of denigrating the *nomos* of Moses. He escapes from doing so by terming the *nomos* of Moses as the best possible imitation of *physis,* contrasting the *nomos* of Moses with the *nomos* of Greek city-states. In the latter, a new king can rescind old laws or introduce new ones; the *nomos* of Moses, though, is eternal and unchangeable. If one moves from Athens to Sparta, the *nomos* changes; the *nomos* of Moses is everywhere the same. Hence, though the *nomos* of Moses seems kindred to the laws of the city-states (both *nomoi* being written, and sensible imitations of intelligible nature), qualitatively the *nomos* of Moses is superior to them and is, indeed, the best possible approximation of *physis.*[2]

In Philo's use of the "unwritten law of nature," he gives central and primary importance to it, rather than to the *nomos* of Moses.

Koester notes, correctly, that Philo, as it were, merges God and *physis* into one:[3] "The law of nature is not an immanent law, but

it is the law of the transcendant creator who rules his creation. . . ." The adjectives which Philo uses for God he also uses
for *physis*. In a word, in Philo the law of nature is God's law:
"The Father and Maker of the world was in the truest sense also
its lawgiver" (*On Moses* II, 48).

Koester asserts that what we have here is "a new concept which
did not exist before in the Hellenistic world," for in Philo "the
Greek notion of an unwritten law is strangely altered . . . since
[the unwritten law] is presented as the result of divine legislation."

What Philo is here doing is making into a synthetic unity an
idea basic to Greek thought, that right reason can arrive at the
fundamental norms of conduct worthy of commendation to men,
with a view basic in Judaism that Scripture divinely reveals these
fundamental norms. Philo is emphasizing the unity of all realms
of human experience,[4] against those views which stress the sense
in which *physis* and *nomos* can be opposites and hence an obstacle
to unity.

Koester goes on to say that "there can be little doubt that Philo
has to be considered as the crucial and most important contribu-
tor to the development of the theory of natural law" which ensued later. "Only a philosophical and theological setting in which
the Greek concept of nature was fused with the belief in a divine
legislator and with a doctrine of the most perfect (written!) law
could produce such a theory, and only here could the Greek
dichotomy of the two realms of law and nature be overcome."

There are two sides to Philo's accomplishment. One is his Hellenization of Judaism in that he presents Scriptural matters in Grecian categories. But the other side is possibly even more important: Philo also Judaizes Grecian ideas. That Philo accomplishes
this double process is the most significant testimony to the profundity of the Hellenization found in the thought of this loyal
Jew. It is a Hellenization not just in form but also in substance.

It has been contended, with some broad agreement on the part of scholars, that Philo both reproduces a great measure of Plato-nism and Stoicism, and distorts them. Professor Wolfson, whose study of Philo concentrates on the philosophy rather than on the "history of religion" aspects of Philo, turns the allegations of dis-tortion into what for him is a great achievement, namely, Philo in these "distortions" is deliberately critical of the philosophical heritage that has come to him. His deliberate bending and alter-ing the ideas of Plato and the Stoics is by no means a result of poor understanding on his part but rather of an incisive and pene-trating understanding and correction of the "errors" in both.

Professor Valentin Nikiprowetzky, a foremost French scholar in Philonic studies, expresses the view that Wolfson has gone much too far in assessing Philo's significance as a philosopher. Yet Nikiprowetzky writes in defense of Philo against his many detractors, doing so through emphasizing what should be self-evident, that Philo's chosen task is to explain Scripture. That is, Philo indeed frequently calls on his vast knowledge of Greek phi-losophy, but it is his explanation of Scripture that controls and determines the philosophy which he uses; the philosophy never controls the explanation. The case is not, as it were, of his reading Plato and the Stoics into Scripture, but rather of his altering facets of Platonism and the Stoics to clarify Scripture. It is Scrip-ture that is sacred for Philo, not Greek philosophy. If, as Niki-prowtzky says, Philo must explain and justify Scripture, whether the plainly literal or at least what Scripture is trying to say, even his allegory has no more than a relative value and is more or less of only momentary significance.[5] Once one abandons an exces-sive preoccupation with the issues of the aptness or ineptness of Philo's philosophy in relation to Plato and the Stoics, the achieve-ment of Philo stands out in its true contours. That achievement is his skill, dedicated insight, and profundity in explaining Scrip-ture, and if Greek thought as Philo inherited it did not do so to his satisfaction, he had no reluctance about bending Greek thought to his purpose.

But the main accomplishment in Philo must stand out: he has blended *physis* and Torah so thoroughly that in his thought they are inextricably bound together.

How shall we delineate a man as complex as Philo? Surely in part he was a philosopher. Surely he was in part a psychologist. Professor Marguerite Harl[6] ascribes to him the achievement of interiorizing religion, and surely this is right.

Can we use the word "mystic" respecting Philo? Some have done so, while others have either abstained from the term or else rejected it respecting Philo. In part the abstention from the term arises from differing conceptions or definitions of mysticism. The rejection of the term for Philo by Walther Völker[7] rests on his contention that its ascription to Philo is motivated by the desire "to discredit Christian mysticism as its very outset by its pretended extra-Christian origin." I fail to see that ascribing mysticism to Philo discredits Christian mysticism. If it is right to call Philo a mystic, to do so is in no way an aspersion on Christianity.

I myself would not call Philo a mystic unless I preceded it with the word philosophical. By this I do not mean only that Philo utilizes philosophy, as obviously he did. Rather, Philo was not an intuitive mystic as I believe Paul was. Philo was given to meditation and contemplation, and his sense of union with God is at all times controlled or even determined by his broad knowledge and his rationalism. His own experience of "seeing the divine vision" is always expressed against such a background.

Moreover, the goal in all that Philo implied in his writing or stated directly is for man to be united with God. What he has set forth as the goal is that which he feels he has himself experienced. Surely the term "philosophical mystic" is justified because it does describe him.

# II

# 9

## Philo and Palestinian Judaism

In a very broad sense, Philo is contemporary with the early development of Synagogue Judaism, this latter a term to be understood in contrast to the Judaism of the Temple in Jerusalem. After the Temple was destroyed by the Romans in A.D. 70, its sacrificial cult was ended, and the role of priests was no longer operative. Synagogue Judaism not only survived the events of 70, but also emerged as the form of Judaism that has persisted to our time. Subsequent to 70, Synagogue Judaism became stabilized and more thoroughly organized as a consequence of developments associated with events in the year 90 at the city called in Greek Jamnia (Yavne in Aramaic). In the next century, that is, by A.D. 200, the accumulated traditions of the Synagogue underwent a transition from the oral to the written. These traditions are known in Judaism as the Oral Torah, a term that has persisted even after the traditions had been written down.

To speak of these traditions as accumulated implies that they represent an extended period of time, either in oral or possibly written form. Some of the traditions are clearly older than Philo. It has therefore been an ordinary facet in the study of Philo to inquire into his relationship to the Oral Torah. There are some

complexities that attend this inquiry, and these will need to be
noted.

First, though, we need to understand certain terms, the use of
which can facilitate our grasp of the issues in this inquiry. Our
initial attention is to the types of literature that arose: by Targum
is meant the translation of Scripture into Aramaic. Next, by the
Midrash is meant an expository explanation of Scripture very
kindred to a commentary on it, and arranged in the sequence of
the Scriptural content, so that one speaks of the Midrash to Exodus, to Numbers, and the like. Third, by Mishna is meant a topi-
cal arrangement of the explanations and expositions of the legal
aspects of Scripture. There is a large measure of overlap in content between the Midrash and the Mishna, for the material is often
the same, the distinction being in the form. Tractates of the
Mishna bear titles such as The Sabbath, Passover, The Day of
Atonement, and the like. Last, the Tosefta, as its translation, "addition," implies, is a kind of supplement to the Mishna; it is an assembly of materials on the topics of the Mishna but which
chanced not to be included in the Mishna.

From a totally different standpoint, two more terms need definition. Where Scripture is narrative, as is the case with Genesis,
the explanation/exposition is largely narrative embellishment. The
term "haggada" is used to describe such embellishments of Scriptural narratives. For example, Scripture relates that Abraham was
born in Ur but left it to go to Charran. Scripture does not tell
why Abraham left. The haggada supplies an answer: Ur was a
center of idolatry, and, indeed, his father owned a shop where
idols were sold. On one occasion Abraham was left in charge of
the shop. He chopped all the idols but the biggest into pieces and
put the hatchet into the hands of the biggest idol. On the return
of his father, he explained that the biggest idol had chopped the
other idols into pieces. It was his desire to be away from the environment of idolatry and astrology that impelled Abraham to
leave Ur.

Haggada, then, is the expansion and embellishment of Scriptural narrative. At times this embellishment is itself a narrative (as is the case with Abraham's chopping the idols to pieces); at times it is a brief embellishment of a Scriptural item but is not presented as a full narrative. For example, when in Gen. 18:1 God appeared to Abraham, it was to pay a sick-call on Abraham, who in chapter 17 had become circumcised.

In contrast to haggada, the term "halacha" is used in connection with laws and commandments. In connection with some requirements, Scripture sets forth a general principle but not the attendant applications; in other instances Scripture sets forth a series of related laws but abstains from providing the basic general principle. "Halacha" is the term used for the legal requirements inferred from Scripture but not explicit in it. The deduction of a general principle from a set of individual requirements or the deduction of a set of individual requirements from a general principle is termed "halachic." There are some other meanings to the word "halacha" that are slightly divergent but similar: Halacha can mean the settled opinion in legal matters in those cases where an unresolved dispute, with varying opinions as to what the halacha should be, has been transmitted. For example, when the Academy of Hillel asserted that the derived law should be X and the Academy of Shammai asserted that it should be Y, then the conclusion as to which view should prevail takes the form of saying "the halacha is in accordance with the viewpoint of the Academy of Hillel." The upshot has been the usual use of the word "halacha" to denote a non-biblical (and post-biblical) requirement, this in contrast to a *mitzva* which is an explicit biblical commandment. The Hebrew word *mitzva*, "commandment," alludes to biblical law, halacha to rabbinic law.

Haggada and halacha to some extent are contained in the Targum; they are the substance of the Midrash and the Mishna. Both haggada and halacha are to be found in Philo. The question is legitimate whether there are some connections between the materials of Philo, an Alexandrian, and the materials that arose in Judea. But how secure can we be that Judean materials recorded at least a century after Philo's time and ascribed to pre-Philonic sages are authentically pre-Philonic? The question arises out of phenomena in the Rabbinic literature, chiefly its lack of concern with historical precision, and hence the possibility that a pre-Philonic dating for some such materials may be only legendary and therefore hazardous. Can we with certainty isolate from later written collections material that is to be classified as exceedingly early? The setting down of the Mishna is dated about A.D. 175–200; can we securely date materials to 20 B.C.? The fact is that we lack the controls for the certainty and precision which we should like to have because the Judean literature does not provide these controls in an unmistakable way.[1]

In the area of haggada we have some rather clear clues respecting such chronological factors. A work known as Jubilees is a retelling of Genesis and a portion of Exodus; it is marked by a great deal of haggadic materials. Though scholars differ in the exact date of the composition of Jubilees, there is a usual agreement that makes it pre-Philonic, that is, between 100 and 50 B.C. Haggadic materials in Jubilees reappear in Josephus, *The Antiquity of the Jews;* Josephus' dates are A.D. 37 to ±100. Moreover, some of these haggadic items that appear in Jubilees are found in the Midrash to Genesis, recorded much later. Chronologically, then, Palestinian haggadic materials could have been available to Philo.[2] The key question, to which we shall return, is whether he actually availed himself of these materials.

There are also halachic items which appear in passing in pre-Philonic writings such as Ecclesiasticus and Tobit. Conceivably halacha had so developed in Palestine by the time of Philo that he could have availed himself of this material, at least as far as chronology is concerned.[3]

The issue can be put in this way: where we find haggadic or halachic materials common to Palestinian collections and to Philo, shall we conclude that Philo derived these from Palestine? If so, then there must have been an adequate measure of communication, and such communication must have overcome the language problem, for the Rabbinic materials are in Hebrew and Aramaic.

Did Philo know Hebrew-Aramaic? It is often asserted, for example, by Harry Wolfson, that since Philo was a Jew, he necessarily knew Hebrew. But a contention of this sort is a pre-judgment and scarcely a proof. What can be mustered in the way of evidence?

The view that Philo knew Hebrew is, as we have said, derived from the abundance of instances in which he gives the meaning of the names in Hebrew of biblical characters and places. Again repeating, often in his giving the meaning, Philo renders the Hebrew correctly. But just as often, the Hebrew is not correctly rendered, and we encounter a capricious translation that can be called incorrect. But granted that Hebrew knowledge, whether accurate or inaccurate, is reflected in the translation of biblical names, it can be legitimately asked whether Philo himself possessed this knowledge. There are inherited from a time later than Philo lists of biblical names and the Hebrew meaning of them. Conceivably such lists that antedated Philo were available to him, though we knew of no such lists that are assuredly pre-Philonic.[4]

On one level the issue of whether Philo knew Hebrew is deemed to be related to the matter of his knowledge and use of the Palestinian haggada and halacha. To assume that he knew Hebrew would suggest such close communication with movements in Palestine that Philo would readily know the halacha and haggada which were there unfolding. If he did not know Hebrew, then possibly he did not actually know the halacha and haggada of Judea; if so, Philo reflects Hellenistic biblical embellishment that was a separate parallel development from Scripture. On another level, the issue of the knowledge of Hebrew is related to the crucial question: was there a substantial difference between Palestinian and Philonic Judaism?

Philo neither quotes nor even mentions any of the books found in the Apocrypha or Pseudepigrapha, though he alludes to the narrative found in the Letter of Aristeas.

It needs to be clear that there are unmistakable overlaps in haggadic and halachic elements between Philo and Palestinian developments. On the one hand, there is no reason to deny two-way communication between Alexandria and Palestine.[5] Yet, on the other hand, if overlaps in haggadic and halachic elements represent independent development from the common Scripture, the quantity of communication would seem less. For example, the common haggadic motif that Noah did not attain the high level of righteousness that Abraham, Isaac, and Jacob attained suggests dependency neither of Philo on the rabbis nor of the rabbis on Philo but on the wording of Scripture that Noah was righteous "in his generation." These last words surely reflect a deliberate intention by the biblical writer to praise Noah, but only with reservations. Moreover, after the flood, Noah had on one occasion fallen into a drunken stupor. Hence, true as it was that Noah was righteous, this was only in comparison with his unrighteous contemporaries. That is to say, it is conceivable that independent but parallel interpretation of a common Scripture produced the overlaps, whether in this item about Noah or in the broader array of overlaps.[6]

Respecting halacha, a substantial study by Bernard Ritter[7] is the basis for the view among some scholars that Philo knew and used the Palestinian halacha. In addition to Ritter's basic work there have been three studies by Samuel Belkin,[8] who purported to have discovered even more instances of halachic overlap than Ritter had set forth. Also Suzanne Daniel[9] believes that she has found Palestinian halacha in Philo. It is significant that Belkin, having presented the material that he had gathered, went on to conclude that there was no real difference between Philonic Judaism and the Palestinian. A bit later we will raise the question of the propriety of Belkin's conclusion, even if a large measure of halachic similarity or identity is conceded. But a very strong denial of any influence of Palestinian influence on Philo is expressed by the great scholar, Isaac Heinemann.[10]

Respecting haggada, whatever overlap exists between Philo and the Rabbis is strictly limited to brief motifs; that is, Philo's haggada never takes the form of anecdotal narratives. To repeat for the purpose of clarity, the Rabbis and Philo overlap in portraying Ur as a center of astrology and idolatry. The motif of Abraham in his father's idol shop is totally absent from Philo. No rabbinic narrative anecdotes at all appear in Philo.

Yet in the Hellenistic Jewish writers, whom Philo probably knew, there are haggadic elements which Philo never reproduces. The best explanation is that, rationalist and "elitist" that he was, he scorned this material. Comparably, it is not at all impossible that Philo knew rabbinic haggadic anecdotes but disdained using them.

The supposed overlaps between Philo and the Rabbis are, in the mind of some students, considerably exaggerated.[11] In my *Philo's Place in Judaism*, I tried to show that what Louis Ginzberg in his *Legends of the Jews* and Harry A. Wolfson in his *Philo* offered as overlaps were as frequently marked by dissimilarity as by similarity. These pseudo-parallels seem to distort both the Rabbis and Philo.[12]

Moreover, in matters of halacha, there is as much disparity as there is overlap, while in the matter of haggada, there is infinitely more disparity than overlap.

A prudent set of conclusions, gleaned from the views of scholars, would be the following. There are overlaps in halacha between Philo and the Rabbis. Communication between Alexandria and Palestine need not be denied. Overlaps, however, do not prove a dependency of Philo on the Rabbis, for often the overlap is between Philo and a Rabbi who flourished long after Philo. Inde-

pendent, parallel developments seem the better explanation than
that of major dependency in either direction.

But even were the items of overlap more abundant, and less
challengeable than they are, such overlap would scarcely justify
the conclusion of Belkin. The distinction which may or may not
exist between Philo and the Rabbis is independent of that of halachic identity. Hasidism of the eighteenth century did not differ
in halacha from the "misnagdim," the opponents of Hasidism.
Halachic identity does not impinge on the distinction between
the "enthusiasm" of the Hasidim and the calm rationalism of the
Misnagdim.

The viewpoint that seems right is not that Philo and the Rabbis
differed essentially in halacha, but that they differed in religiosity
as between Philo's philosophic mysticism and the non-mystic,
non-philosophic manner of the Rabbis. Philo's philosophical mysticism is essentially Grecian. If we ascribe Jewishness to the Rabbis alone, then Philo is essentially not Jewish. But, to repeat, no
Jew in history ever surpassed Philo in loyalty to Judaism. Philo
often quotes Plato and other Greeks, but he wrote no treatises on
Pythagoras, or Plato, or Aristotle. The treatises he wrote were on
Abraham, Joseph, and Moses. There is no persuasive evidence
that he clearly knew and abundantly utilized Palestinian exegesis.
But nevertheless the Hellenization in him is a Hellenization of Judaism, not of some other religious tradition.

# 10

## Philo and Gnosticism

A "gnostic" was a man who "knew," who knew the way to God through personal illumination. Gnostics came to considerable prominence in the second century church, to the displeasure of what we might call an emerging orthodoxy. Why the displeasure? Because a gnostic, assured of personal illumination, could arise to challenge the tranquility of the developing church, and the authority of its leaders. Gnostics in the area of doctrine tended to stress their personal illumination as over and against church tradition in which there was emphasis on the events that had taken place in church experience. Thus, gnostics tended to deny the historical events which church tradition transmitted relating to Jesus, specifically that Jesus had actually been a man; it was the gnostic view that Jesus, a spirit, had been an apparition, and not truly a man. Why this denial of history? Because gnostics were extreme dualists who scorned anything and everything physical, in the extremity of their dualism. In the mainstream of Christian contentions was the assertion that its claims were right because they rested on reports of witnesses of the events which had taken place. The Gospel According to Matthew was regarded as having been written by a disciple of Jesus; the Gospel

According to John at 21:24 suggests that its author had personally seen the events he had described and hence they were true.
The gnostics in effect denied that the events narrated about Jesus
had happened, and repudiated the testimonies to them.

A second basis for Christian contentions was that Scripture
(that is, the Old Testament) had foretold the events destined to
occur. Especially in the Epistles of Paul and the Gospel According to Matthew, Scripture is quoted to buttress the Christian
claims. The gnostic dualism, with its preoccupation with the evil
believed resident in this world, denied that God could have created it. Rather, God had created a demi-urge, an artisan god, who
had done the creation. Genesis begins with the account of God's
creation of this world, and in chapter one the refrain is repeated
that "God saw and behold it was good." But this world is manifestly evil; hence Genesis is not true but false. Some gnostics,
sharing in a weird admiration for Moses which had spread into
the Gentile world, proceeded to scorn Scripture by asserting that
the great Moses had not written the Five Books of Moses; rather,
it was demons who were the author. In effect such gnostics were
asserting that Christianity was a new movement, devoid of any
rooting in Judaism; the usual Christian view was to the contrary,
namely, that Christianity was the True Israel, the legatee of the
promises to patriarchs in Scripture, and, in effect, Christianity
was as old as the age of the patriarchs.

Until the rise towards the end of the nineteenth century of the
"history of religions" approach, gnosticism was regarded as a
strictly Christian phenomenon of the second Christian century.
The great church historian Adolf von Harnack had described
gnosticism as the end result of the complete "hellenization of the
Gospel." But scholars representing the history of religions, inquiring more deeply into the phenomenon of gnosticism, raised the
issue of whether there might have been a pre-Christian, non-
Christian gnosticism which thereafter entered into Christianity.

There were those who affirmed that a pre-Christian gnosticism had existed; there were others who denied its existence.

Much of the debate centered originally on the Gospel According to John. On the one hand, passages such as John 20:24–27 which portray doubting Thomas as seeing the wounds in Jesus' body and touching Jesus were used for a prevalent view that in part John is a polemics against gnostics in the church. On the other hand, Rudolf Bultmann, in his commentary on John, has set forth that the prologue ("In the beginning was the Logos and the Logos was with God . . .") was derived from an earlier gnostic hymn and adopted by John into his Gospel. Bultmann's view rested on the assumption that there did exist a pre-Christian non-Christian gnosticism. Critics of Bultmann noted correctly that we have not inherited any such gnostic literary precursor to the prologue to John, and that Bultmann was quite unable to cite such a precursor.

The debate over gnosticism has gone on for almost a century. In part it has persisted through a semantic confusion. At a conference held in Messina, Italy,[1] a document was drawn up with the purpose of ending the confusion, by the proposal to use the term *gnosis* for the pre-Christian phenomenon and to reserve "gnosticism" for the second-century Christian phenomenon.[2]

A foremost scholar, Hans Jonas, has set forth what to his mind is the necessary content before some manifestation deserved to be called "gnosticism." In context, he would not classify as gnostic "a Gnosticism without a fallen god, without benighted creator and sinister creation, without alien soul, cosmic captivity and acosmic salvation, without the self-redeeming of the Deity—in short: a Gnosis without divine tragedy will not meet specifications."[3]

Where does Philo stand in this matter? Obviously, if by gnosticism the second-century Christian phenomenon is meant, then

Philo would be irrelevant except as a vague precursor. But if gnosis was earlier than Christianity, aspects of Philonism could have an affinity with it. I wrote respecting this matter as it affects Philo: "I see no trace of a fallen god; I see, however, the logos as the creator. As to a sinister creation, I see in Philo the view that this world of appearance is rather sinister, and that the sage is indeed an alien soul in this world. I do not see cosmic captivity or acosmic salvation; I do see salvation of the soul from the prison of the body. I do not wonder at the absence of a fallen god, for Philo was a staunch Jew; in the light of Genesis I, and the repeated refrain of 'God saw and it was good,' Philo would scarcely admit of a benighted creator. Philo was a dualist, antagonistic to the body with its senses and passions; how extreme a dualist is he? Compared with Christian gnostics, his dualism was not extreme; compared with the rabbis in the normative tradition, it was extreme."

Rather curiously, Erwin R. Goodenough, who regarded Philo as thoroughly Hellenized, saw no relation between Philo and Gnosis. He wrote[4] that Philo "would . . . have had no sympathy with that travesty of philosophy, the type of mythological presentation to which we give the collective name of Gnosticism." One suspects that Goodenough had in mind Christian gnosticism, not *gnosis*. There could seem to be some connection between the intellectual defense of the Greek mysteries and *gnosis*, but as yet very little has been written on the topic. This is possibly due to the rather scant surviving literature, both of *gnosis* and of the mysteries.

I would not myself ever describe Philo as a gnostic. Others speak of him as a proto-gnostic.[5] I would rather stress that in many ways he stands close to *gnosis*, but one always needs to recall Philo's unique elitism and individualism, and to keep him apart from irrational approaches or from folk motifs. I doubt that there was in Philo's time enough of a gnostic entity that could be called a movement. And if there had been such, I doubt that he would have been part of it. That as early as Philo there existed tendencies that eventuated in gnosticism seems possible. But these were at most sporadic,[6] a phenomenon of individuals, and not anything that could be called a movement.

# II

## Goodenough on Philo

That Philo's religiosity is basically different from that of the ancient Rabbis is a viewpoint held by a substantial number of eminent scholars. Within this number of scholars the viewpoint of Goodenough represents quite an extreme. An exposition of Goodenough's viewpoint is significant in itself, but it is also of importance in grasping the way in which the discipline of "the history of religions" has been applied to the Philonic material.

The phrase "history of religions" is awkward. It arose in the English-speaking world by the translation of a German term, *Religionsgeschichte*. What do the English phrase and the German term mean?

The supposition behind *Religionsgeschichte*—History of Religions—is that the phenomena of religion should be studied with scientific detachment and in great breadth and depth. By contrast, pious study of the documents of a particular religion has often been for the purpose of aggrandizing that religion and of edifying its communicants; such study, however profound, has also often been narrow in vision in that such scholarship has confined itself to the documents sacred to the tradition without substantial attention to related materials found in extraneous sources.

Because traditional religions, Judaism and Christianity for example, make claims of uniqueness in quality, scholars in these traditions have made claims of a total uniqueness in content, thereby setting these two religions apart from other religious movements and from relevant literature of the time. The claim of History of Religions is that it is a discipline that is broader and more objective than traditional learning.

Earliest Christianity was born in Aramaic-speaking Judaism. It spread beyond the borders of Judea and became altered into a Greek-speaking entity. No Aramaic documents of early Christianity have survived; all of the New Testament was transmitted in Greek. While occasional theories have sporadically been expressed that this or that book of the New Testament is a translation of an Aramaic composition, it is the almost unanimous view of New Testament scholars that the New Testament writings are Greek compositions, not translations. The transition in the language of early Christianity from Aramaic to Greek is viewed as a phenomenon of the Oral period, and was consummated prior to the writing of the documents in Greek.

The earliest writings in the New Testament are the Epistles of Paul, written in Greek and addressed to Greek-speaking readers. These Epistles are usually regarded as having been composed in the period from about A.D. 40 to A.D. 55, the period of Paul's missionary activity.

The precise date of the death of Jesus and the rise of the belief in his resurrection is unknown. Christian tradition, reflected in the Gospels, ascribes his death to the term in which Pontius Pilate served as the "procurator" (governor) of Judea; the dates of his term are known from Josephus as A.D. 26–36. Presumably the death of Jesus occurred within that span of time; many scholars select the date of 29 for the death of Jesus, but some prefer 30, some 31, and some 33. If Paul's activity as the divinely chosen apostle to the Gentiles began as early as 40, that is, a decade or less after the death of Jesus, then surely the Greek Epistles of

Paul suggest that a Hellenization of Christianity took place very soon and very rapidly. How can we account for the quick and rapid Hellenization of Christianity? In the early nineteenth century the view was expressed that Hellenized Judaism had prepared the way, and made possible the rapid Hellenization of Christianity.[1] That view became part of Goodenough's more encompassing approach.

It was a hope of Goodenough early in his career to write a history of the growth and development of Christianity. In his travels in the Mediterranean world, he saw in the catacombs at Rome and Monteverde the mural paintings that were ascribed to Christian artists of the second Christian century. It puzzled Goodenough that developed Christian art could have flourished so early. He wondered if there might have been a Jewish art which prepared the way for the Christian art and which accounted for its rapid flourishing. Yet there was unanimous written testimony from the Rabbis, Philo, and Josephus that pictorial art was forbidden Jews. Goodenough wondered if there might have been some marginal versions of Judaism which were not averse to pictorial art.

While Goodenough was wondering about this possibility, some of his colleagues at Yale were excavating a site in Syria known as Dura Europos. There they uncovered a synagogue whose walls were covered with paintings. Persuaded by this discovery that there was indeed evidence for marginal Jewries for whom pictorial art was not tabu, Goodenough began a renewed study of Philo's writings with the premise that Philo reflected a marginal Judaism, different in essentials from all previously-known versions of Judaism. He called his first book in this area *By Light, Light: The Mystical Gospel of Hellenistic Judaism*.

It was Goodenough's view that Philo represented a Hellenization so complete that the Jewish elements in Philo were only a shadowy background. While it is true that Philo scorned and attacked the Greek mystery religions, the Judaism of Philo is itself,

according to Goodenough, a Greek mystery religion. Goodenough did not mean thereby, as some outraged critics contended,
that Philo had borrowed the rites and practices of the Greek
cults; rather, as Goodenough saw matters, Philo's approach to Judaism was kindred to that of pagan intellectuals such as Plutarch
in their approach to the pagan mysteries. It was, then, not rites or
ceremonies that Philo borrowed from his Hellenistic environment but thought-patterns and motifs.[2]

Two such motifs, as previously isolated in the History of Religions, were the "light stream"[3] and the great feminine principle
of the "great mother." According to both of these motifs, man is
alone in a hostile world, seeking "escape" from it; such escape is
"salvation." The light-stream stems from the transcendent godhead, and, radiating down, illumines the prospective initiate into
the mystery, thereby uniting him with the divine light and providing him with salvation and immortality. Goodenough showed
how abundantly Philo utilized the motif of the light-stream.
Comparably, the motif of the "great mother" does the same
thing. In several passages in Philo,[4] Sarah (equivalent to the
"great mother") was allegorically true wisdom, and hence virgin
(see pp. 114–15). Abraham was not the father of Isaac; rather,
God was the father, Sarah was the virgin mother who bore Isaac
("spiritual joy"), whom she then presented to the patriarch
Abraham.

The function of the Greek mysteries was to furnish to initiates
the salvation they could not attain on their own. While Philo on
the one hand does make provision for the supremely gifted to attain salvation on their own, for most Jews the Laws of Moses
were the vehicle by which the ordinary Jew achieved this result.
The literal Laws were described in Philo's approach by Goodenough as representing the lower mystery, the "mystery of
Aaron"; the allegory of the Laws enabled one to enter into the
higher mystery, the "mystery of Moses." It is universally acknowledged, even by Goodenough's opponents, that Philo utilizes

terms common in the Greek mysteries, such as initiation, illumination, and perfection.[5] The issue raised by opponents of Goodenough was whether Philo was doing anything more than merely utilizing the terminology, without really adopting the content. For example, Wolfson, who regarded Philo as a usual Jew, conceded that Philo used the terms of the mysteries, but he insisted that Philo meant nothing significant thereby.

In further pursuit of delineating Philo's religiosity, Goodenough suggested a contrast between "objective" religion and "subjective." In objective religion, the communicant faithfully executes the demands of the religion, yet without any personal and vivid sense of communion with God. In subjective religion, the observance of the demands of the religion is taken for granted, but the nub of religion is the experience of communion.[6]

In proposing the possibility of Judaism's having been transformed into a mystery, Goodenough aroused opposition kindred to that aroused by those interpreters who had viewed early Christianity as a mystery religion. The mere suggestion in both cases was responded to with resentment, as if the suggestion was in itself the utmost in denigration. The rejection of the suggestion respecting Christianity had been expressed with unlimited heat. Such too was the response to Goodenough. It was not readily discerned by such offended critics that Goodenough was trying to describe a phenomenon, not debase Judaism.

Goodenough's further writings on Philo represented his efforts to document the uniqueness of Philo's Judaism, as contrasted with Rabbinic Judaism. Repeatedly Goodenough proclaimed his lament that his own linguistic limitations prevented his dealing at first hand with Rabbinic texts and his need to rely on translations of them. There were scholars who condescendingly dismissed Goodenough out of hand simply because he was not able to read Rabbinic texts in the original.[7]

Becoming all the more deeply persuaded that there were marginal Judaisms which differed at essential points from Rabbinic Judaism, Goodenough then turned to symbols found on Jewish tombstones and in the mosaics in Jewish synagogues, this for the purpose of explaining the meaning of the symbols: the candelabrum, the ram's horn, the rosettes, the fish, the ship. In his thirteen-volume work, *Jewish Symbols in the Greco-Roman Period*, 1953 ff., he collected and reproduced these symbols with all the thoroughness possible.

For the most part there is no legacy of writing from the Greco-Roman period by which to explain the meaning of the symbols. How then can a modern literary explanation arise for non-literary representations? Goodenough found his way out of the dilemma by recourse to the theories of Carl Jung. Stated briefly, Jung held that folk memory preserved man's basic drives and needs which had arisen in man's pre-historic age; these preserved impulses manage to take on, with the passing of time, both pictorial and literary form, which were conditioned by the age and environment. But behind the pictorial and the literary of some given age are the basic, universal impulses preserved from pre-historic man.[8]

Once in a seminar—I know of no published version of this—Goodenough chose the Jewish Passover as an example of the primordial on the one hand and the later pictorial or literary expression on the other. Scripture preserves in Lev. 23:5–6 a distinction, which in time disappeared, between the pastoral "passover" and the "agricultural" feast of unleavened bread. Both were spring festivals. The pastoral celebrated the renewal of life through the birth of lambs, one of which needed to be sacrificed to the Deity so that the many newborn lambs could be retained. The feast of unleavened bread celebrated the renewal of life through the newly-grown grain, which needed to be harvested and quickly baked into flat, unleavened cakes. In time the separate festivals merged into one.

The literary enters in in that Scripture had prescribed the

slaughter of a lamb and the eating of unleavened bread as a memorial of God's saving act in freeing the Hebrews from their enslavement in Egypt. The primordial impulse behind the festival was to observe the renewal of life in the spring. That the lamb and the unleavened bread celebrated supposed historical events, known to men's consciousness, was a literary way of expressing a very ancient primordial impulse buried in the unconsciousness in man. Moreover, modern Jews, including those who deny the history of the enslavement in Egypt and of the supernatural release, find value in attending a Passover seder. This value, according to Goodenough, arises from an unconscious identification, even by sophisticated modern people, with the primordial impulses of prehistoric man. Again, Christianity altered the Passover into Easter. The renewal of life, in the resurrection of Jesus, is still another form of the persistence in the folk memory from the primordial age, despite constantly changing forms of expressions such as arose in later ages and geographical settings.

The Jewish symbols in the Greco-Roman period, according to Goodenough, are never merely decorative. They are always mystic symbols—that is, symbols of man's yearning to be united with God. Some of these Jewish symbols—the ship, for example[9]—have a pagan origin. But whether the symbols are of Jewish origin or Jewish adoptions of pagan symbols, the Judaism where these symbols were used mystically was a marginal Judaism.

Goodenough's views[10] have been opposed both respecting details and in toto. The primary rejection has rested on the basis that his concept of marginal Judaisms is without substance. It has been contended that the inner divisions in Judaism, exemplified by the Pharisees and the Sadducees, fall short of justifying a distinction between "normative" Judaism and a supposedly marginal form of it.

Wolfson's *Philo* was published in 1947, after Goodenough's major studies on Philo, but before Goodenough's *Jewish Sym-*

*bols in the Greco-Roman Period.* It v as not set forth as a rejection of Goodenough, but that is what in large measure it is. Wolfson describes Philo's Judaism as a "collateral form of Pharisaism." Wolfson repeatedly characterizes some Philonic passage as a reflection of an item already current in "native, Palestinian Judaism." As to Hebrew, Wolfson believes that Philo knew Hebrew; he asserts that the burden of proof rests on those who deny that knowledge, rather than on those who affirm it. He sets forth that the "unwritten law" in Philo, which others took as a Stoic doctrine, was nothing other than the "Oral Torah" of the Pharisees. That is, Wolfson and Goodenough are a hundred and eighty degrees apart.

My own viewpoint can be stated in the following way: I believe that those who regard Philo as thoroughly Hellenized are right, and that Wolfson is wrong. But I believe also that Goodenough represents a viewpoint that is guilty of excess and that, fascinating as his views are, they are all too often insubstantial.[11] I have serious reservations about the validity of interpreting the pictorial by modern theories of psychoanalysis.

But I believe too that Goodenough is right in the view that Hellenized Judaism, represented by Philo, made possible the rapid Hellenization of Christianity.

Yet caution is important: Philo reflects Hellenized Judaism, but at the same time he is in many ways unique within that entity we can call Hellenistic Judaism. He is almost as remote from the Hellenistic Judaism of the Greco-Jewish writers whom we know from the fragments in Eusebius as he is from the Judaism of Midrash and Talmud. It is not wrong to regard Philo as representing a marginal *viewpoint*. But I have seen no evidence that Philo speaks for a segment of Jewry large enough to be called a *marginal Judaism*.

# 12

## Philo and Christianity

Since the New Testament literature is Greek and arises from outside Judea, its common geographical and linguistic characteristics with Philo can reasonably lead us to expect reflections of Philo in aspects of New Testament literature and thought. This would seem especially to be the case if we conceive of Hellenistic Judaism as an entity different from both Palestinian Judaism and Hellenistic paganism, sharing some elements with both but yet distinctive from them.[1] Central to Hellenistic Judaism was its loyalty to Scripture in the Greek version. Various levels of education and economic and local social conditions would have marked Hellenistic Jews, and inner difference among such Jews were inevitable.

One motif of great significance in Hellenistic Judaism and Hellenistic Christianity is that of "wisdom." We have seen that Philo's logos idea has a dual ancestry, the Jewish *hokma* and the Greek *sophia*.[2] In recent scholarship, both in Old and New Testament, there has been a high emphasis on the "wisdom" tradition, and a vast literature now exists.[3] A range of related ideas had come into being which utilized biblical passages, such as Prov. 8: 22–31, to assert, first, that God had himself utilized wisdom in his acts of creation; next, wisdom was an entity potentially available to man as well as to God; and, indeed, wisdom was capable of being personified (as in Proverbs, chapter 8), or, beyond that, conceived of as a "hypostasis," a discrete entity. The idea in hypostasis was that wisdom was truly capable of acting and of doing. In Philo, the Divine Logos, as we saw, was that facet of God which acted in connection with this world, while God in his essence was over and beyond this world. Neither the Logos, nor the Logos plus the "powers," represented the *pleroma* ("fullness") of God, since God was more than these aspects of divine activity.

In the unfolding views found in Christian literature there are some general echoes of the conception of God as over and above this world, and of the Christ as more or less equivalent to the Logos. The direct identification of Logos and Christ occurs in the prologue to the Gospel According to John. Yet there is a necessary prelude that needs to be emphasized. The Logos in Jewish writings, such as Wisdom of Solomon and Philo, is distinct from Christian views in that in the Jewish writings, Logos is what we might call a timeless idea; the Logos in Christian thought is always connected with the *event* of Jesus. That is, on a historic occasion, the Logos, in John's words, became incarnate in Jesus. Hence, while similarities exist in the Christian form of the exposition of the nature of God, there is this difference: Philo's effort is to set forth the philosophical conceptions, while the Christian effort is to fit the *event* of the Christ into its unfolding views.

Still another difference within the context of similarity is to be noted. Philo was a diligent student, an erudite master of the Greek philosophic tradition antecedent to him. A person such as Paul was not a student in this sense; Paul's philosophical knowledge came to him from the atmosphere and not from some diligent poring over texts. One might say, especially respecting Colossians and Ephesians, that these reflect the need to fit the Christ into the general religious ideas of the time, whereas Philo is concerned to provide a pedantic explanation of these general ideas. .

Finally, there is a motif we have seen in Philo in which he liquidates history, exemplified in his denial at the end of *On Mating* that Sarah and Hagar are real women. In the later literature of the New Testament, such as John, the Pastoral Epistles, and First John, there are under attack certain Christian views which dissolve the Christ event into mere symbol. There is, of course, no connection between Philo's unhistorical views and those of "heretical" Christians; what there is in common is the substitution of symbol for event and "existential" response for the legacy of history.

There is an abundance of literature[4] that links Philo and Paul together. At one extreme, rejected by all other scholars I have read, is a view that asserts that Paul had read Philo.[5] Wrong as the statement seems to be, it nevertheless underscores how the two echo each other, not from direct literary dependence but rather out of a common atmosphere. This overlap is to be found in the Epistles of Paul, not in the Acts of the Apostles. The portrait of Paul, as found in Acts, is a very old problem in New Testament scholarship; for our present purposes, it is the Paul of the Epistles alone that is here under consideration.[6]

As to the elements in common, both Philo and Paul have a view of God as fully transcendent and therefore both faced the need to bridge that gap. In both there is found a dualism[7] in which man is composed of a material side which by assumption is evil and an immaterial side which by assumption is good. In both, man is challenged to rise above body and to live in the "intelligible world," as Philo phrases it, or in the "spirit" as Paul does. We need, though, to note some differences that affect at least how each expresses his characteristic views, even if they are basically similar. Thus, Philo was fully a rationalist, Paul not. Paul lived in a universe controlled or inhabited by the devil and governed by principalities; these ideas are not expressed in Philo at all.

For both there existed somewhat similar problems in the Law of Moses. For both the origin of the problem lies in the very name, the *Nomos,* with its inevitable association with courts and judges. Philo, as we saw, needed to strain to justify the presence in the *Nomos* of the Book of Genesis with its relative absence of laws. On a different level, the problem for both is that the Laws are presented only in Exodus, raising the question of the relation of the patriarchs who flourished before Moses to the laws inaugurated in his time. Briefly stated, Philo and Paul have it in common that the patriarchs in Genesis are regarded as the true norm of proper religion, and the laws in Exodus and following books needed in some way to be related to that true norm. Philo's answer, to repeat, was that Genesis was the book of the Law of Nature, and the Mosaic Laws the best possible imitation of it. Philo argues that whoever moves from hope to repentance to tranquility can then elect to proceed further on the road to salvation. Paul knew no such tranquility, and he denied that man can elect to proceed to salvation; he denies that man, on his own and unaided, can reach salvation. Philo is certain that man is able to observe the laws; Paul, that man is unable. Moreover, in Paul's view, the observance is futile, since observance implies that man is relying on himself, not God. In Philo a man, under providence, merits reward or punishment for his deeds; in Paul man cannot work his own salvation but needs to have salvation divinely wrought for him. In Paul the saved are those whom God has predestined for salvation.

Both solve the problem of God's transcendence in similar ways. The terms central to each are different, the key word in Philo being the Logos, while in Paul it is the Christ. In more than one sense the two diverse terms are synonymous, for both terms suggest the mechanism whereby the transcendent God becomes immanent. Yet despite this vague similarity, there is an acute difference. In Philo all is static, and history of little import, since in Philo the Logos is timeless and unconnected with time or space;

in Paul, as already suggested, event is the crucial matter in that the Christ became Jesus in Judea in the immediate past history, and then the Christ appeared to Paul. Though Philo reports that recurrently the Logos had permeated his being, there is a noticeable difference in the way in which the Christ enters into Paul, almost constantly permeates him, and alters him.

There is no echo in Philo of the Pauline doctrine of salvation only by faith. Yet the salvation which both Philo and Paul seek is the same, namely, release from the bondage to the flesh, release from "this world," and release from death. They both use terms found in the Greek mysteries. It might be stated, if only tentatively, that their use of the terminology of the mysteries is connected with their common need to explain the inner psyche of man in connection with such release. Granted that in Paul the Christ event is the most central item, the nature of man respecting his inner life is obviously connected with this matter of release. Erwin R. Goodenough's essay, "Law in the Subjective Realm,"[8] though difficult to read, is well worth the effort. Goodenough asks, what in Paul's mind is the meaning of *dikaiosyne*, "justice," in Paul's contention that man is "justified" (that is, brought to *dikaiosyne*) by faith? Goodenough asserts that the longing for inner peace and salvation was as strong in the religious realm as it was in the political and social realm, and the achievement of inner peace and salvation is carried in the word *dikaiosyne*. When a city-state, through proper governing and proper laws, achieves stability, tranquility, and prosperity, then one can say that *dikaiosyne* prevails there. One needs, though, to notice that proper governing and proper laws are only a precursor to stability and tranquility. The achievement of the admirable state of affairs requires a balance within the various parts of the city-state, in conformity with law; similarly, the achievement of inner peace by an individual requires a balance within the parts of his body. *Dikaiosyne* is not law, but is the end result of proper law. For Philo the "polis" of corporate society was only an imitation, as it were, of the polis in the soul of the individual. Just as a monarch rules the city-state/polis, so the *nous hegemōn*, the "reigning mind," rules the individual.

This reigning mind is the higher of man's two minds. The lower mind receives and sorts out the impressions provided by the senses; the higher mind, possessing reason, moves on to form conclusions, generalizations, and concepts from what the lower mind has assembled. In one direction, then, the senses move on towards the lower mind, and from there there is further motion to the higher mind; conversely, the higher mind directs and controls the lower mind and the senses. *Dikaiosyne* is the result of the control by the higher mind of the lower mind and the senses. What is stated so far in this paragraph is a very much simplified version of what in Philo is inordinately fuller, entailing an abundance of details in Philo's repeated exposition. These are not always presented by Philo in the same way, nor, as scholars have suggested, with fullest consistency.[9]

The *nous hegemōn*, the higher mind, possessing reason, enables a man to live by the law of nature. This, according to Goodenough, is the context for the words of Paul in Romans 7:21-23 as Goodenough presents them: "I find then the law that, to me who would do *ton kalon* (the beautiful), evil is present. For 'I' delight in the law of God after the inward man: but I see a different law in my members, warring against the law of my *nous* ("mind") and bringing me into captivity under the law of sin which is in my members."[10]

There is more detail that Goodenough presents, especially in support of his view of Philo's transformation of Judaism as a mystery, as is set forth in Chapter 11, but we do not here need that detail.

A posthumous essay by Goodenough, completed by his former research assistant, Professor A. T. Kraabel, called "Paul and the Hellenization of Christianity"[11] in many places returns to the same theme set forth in "Law in the Subjective Realm." Aspects of this essay do not need to concern us directly (such as the justification for preferring the Epistles for information about Paul, and for ignoring the portrait of Paul in Acts). In this essay, Goodenough reviews much of the content of Romans, chapters 1–12, extending into his discussion the kernel of his interpretation given above of Rom. 7:21–23. That is to say, Goodenough views the anthropology of Paul, the issues of evil, the meaning of faith, and the virtues as analogous to these matters in Philo. Goodenough is acutely aware of the relative brevity of Romans, and the lack of accord in modes of expression between Paul and Philo. What Goodenough is most constrained to show is that Paul cannot be understood through the sources found in Rabbinic literature;[12] it is Philo whose thought makes Paul's view intelligible, for the similarities are basic and thorough-going. Those scholars who are not prepared to set aside the Paul of Acts will, of course, not subscribe to Goodenough's view, whether in detail or in toto, for Acts, as is to be recalled, presents Paul as something of a Jerusalemite, a student of Gamaliel, and an undeviatingly faithful observer of the laws of Moses. A view which is the direct opposite of Goodenough's is found in W. D. Davies, *Paul and Rabbinic Judaism: Some Rabbinic Elements in Pauline Theology.*[13]

One additional comment. There is in Paul an apocalyptic element, exemplified in II Corinthians, chapter 12, which is in sharp contrast to the absence of that element in Philo.[14] The presence of the apocalyptic in Paul is not decisive for either a Hellenistic or a Palestinian background, for the background for apocalyptic could be either. Whenever Paul and Philo are compared, it is necessary also to present the differences.

We shall deal below with Colossians, the Pauline authorship of which is disputed.

The New Testament writing that has yielded the most abundant literature on possible relations with Philo is the Gospel According to John. As is known, the prologue to the Gospel utilizes the word "Logos"; in the Epistles of Paul where the genuineness of Paul's authorship is not disputed, the word does not appear, though the identification of Christ with Logos seems implicit. It is the explicit identification in John that has yielded the harvest of so much literature, with both theories of a direct dependency of John on Philo[15] and fervent denials of even an indirect dependency. The problem is complicated by the diversity of views on the Gospel, for example, that which regards the Logos prologue as permeating the entire Gospel, and a contrary view which regards the prologue as if it were engrafted onto the Gospel and thereafter forgotten.

There is rather universal agreement, within the controversies, that the Logos prologue is better illumined by an understanding of the Logos idea in Philo than by any other non–New Testament writing; it is agreed that Philo is by far the largest available source for the idea contained in the word Logos. The caution is nevertheless necessary that, as is the case of Paul, John associates the Logos with event, that is, the Logos on a historical occasion became incarnate in the man Jesus, while in Philo the Logos is never brought into relationship with history in this way.

Excessive conclusions can be dangerous. A modest statement can go along the following lines: Philo does have a statement touching on incarnation, this in connection with the three "visitors" to Abraham in Genesis, chapter 18. Philo speaks of them as divine beings incarnate as men, in *Abr.* 118. Less specifically, one might infer incarnation in that Philo views the patriarchs as *nomoi empsychoi*, "laws incarnate in men," and views Moses allegorically as the Logos. But at best such Philonic ideas do not really deal with direct incarnation; they contribute to the atmosphere in which John lived, but without reflecting a direct influence of Philo on him.

Repeatedly the view arises that a term, *memra*, utilized in the Targum, the Aramaic translation of Scripture, has some relation-

ship to Philo. *Memra* means "word"; Logos is often—indeed too
often!—translated as "word." Accordingly, *memra* and logos are
regarded as related, or synonymous, or even identical. But *memra*,
where used in the Targum, is a device of a euphemistic kind, and
part of a motif of broader use: the Targum, with less than complete consistency, tends to eliminate anthropomorphisms and an-
thropopathisms found in the Hebrew text. (Anthropomorphism
means the depicting of God as if he has a human form, such as
his seeing or hearing; anthropopathism means the depicting of
God as if he has human passions, such as anger or joy.) The Targum often resorts to paraphrase rather than to direct translation
so as to reduce or eliminate these factors. Thus, repeatedly when
the Hebrew text tells that God did some deed, the Targum renders the text that the *memra* of God did it. But in the Targum
there is no reflection of the philosophical overtones in Logos as
the immanent aspect of the transcendent God; rather, the Targum is engaging in euphemism, not in philosophical issues. The
connection between *memra* and logos, if any, is at most very
tenuous.

In reference to the Logos prologue, as we mentioned above,
p. 137, Rudolf Bultmann, in his commentary on John, expressed
the view that the prologue was originally a gnostic hymn to the
Logos and that John had not created it but rather borrowed and
adopted it. To repeat, a good many scholars have objected that
Bultmann could not and did not cite any literary source for such
a gnostic hymn; there is, so it has been said, no source other than
Bultmann's speculation.[16] Still other objectors went on to deny
the Hellenistic character of the Gospel. This denial has rested in
part in assertions of the following kind: dualism is found in the
Dead Sea Scrolls sectarian writings; dualism is hence as readily
Jewish and Semitic as Hellenistic; John is an essentially Jewish
gospel. The extreme in this position is that taken by William F.
Albright. His view[17] was that John, usually considered by Christian scholars to be the latest Gospel was in fact the earliest and

was written in Judea, and was Palestinian, not Hellenistic. Albright also believed that the long discourses in John were the authentic words of Jesus.

Remote in detail from Albright, yet susceptible to here being coupled with him, is Martin Hengel.[18] His thesis, presented with an abundance of erudition, is that all of Judea and the writings there composed, even including Rabbinic literature, is influenced, or permeated, or even shaped by Hellenism. It is a thesis that is startling, and one that has evoked a good bit of resistance. A sequel to the book was the appearance of writings which abandoned Hengel's restraint and prudence. Hengel created a great measure of semantic confusion, and occasioned other lamentable sequels, such as the assertion by Howard C. Kee[19] that the division of Jewish and Christian writings into the Judean and the Hellenistic was an untenable scholarly construct. While the student needs to be aware of the viewpoints here cited, he can be reasonably assured that to search in Palestinian Judaism for backgrounds to John, rather than in Hellenistic writings, is to prefer the remote and the marginal rather than the omnipresent and explicit.

The manner of John is surely not identical with that of Philo. Thus, John does not utilize the specific Philonic expressions, "sensible world" and "intelligible world." Yet precisely such a contrast is present and, indeed, it constitutes the chief form of presentation in John. In manner John repeatedly first presents examples of misunderstanding, followed by a correction by Jesus, and thereafter a discourse by him. The misunderstanding is the result of taking such things as rebirth, or bread, or water literally; the correction is that true rebirth, true bread, or true water is always spiritual. The discourse then identifies Jesus and the spiritual entity.

Perhaps this Johannine contrast between the material and the spiritual is a development from an earlier contrast, found in Judaism and in the Synoptic gospels, between this age (a miserable

one!) and the blessed future age. At first this contrast seems to
have been thought of in terms of linear time, between a now and
what is to be in the future when all is altered and a new age will
dawn. The Jewish eschatological views regarding "the end of
time," as in Isaiah 2:2 and Micah 4:1, were linear. But as centuries passed, the blessed future failed to come and the blessed
was manifestly remote, destined for a far-distant future. When
would-be messiahs arose, the contention was that the blessed future was not at all remote, but, happily, it was now near at hand.
But the frustration of messianic expectations led to a partial, or
even complete, abandonment of linear time. A view arose that the
"world to come" was disengaged from time. Rather, the world to
come was viewed as universally available, and immediately so,
and capable of entrance by an individual on his death. The world
to come, then, was a present reality, existing in heaven, in the setting of a heavenly Eden. It was to this heavenly paradise that the
patriarchs had gone after their death; Luke (16:19–31) tells of
Abraham there, welcoming Lazarus to his bosom; in the Rabbinic
literature a sage, on dying and leaving his academy on earth, ascended to the "academy on high." In a sense, the future world
was altered by non-philosophical minds into something that is
vaguely similar to the intelligible world, yet is still quite different
from it. John, though, proceeds far beyond such alteration, for he
seems to shun both futurity and also eschatology; if they are at all
present in his Gospel, as some assert, it is by implication and never
by explicit statement. That "my kingship is not of this world" is
only one of a number of passages in which this world and a
higher one are set into sharp contrast. The profundity in John is
the result of a triumph of his content over the naiveté of the device of misunderstanding, correction, and discourse.

There is a curious set of correspondences: the Synoptic Gospels and the Rabbinic Literature are replete with parables and
pithy folk-statements (such as "if salt loses its savor . . ."). John
and Philo are without parable and pithy statement. A student of

mine, responding to this equation, said, "John seems to Philonize Mark, Matthew, and Luke." I responded that there was more wrong with his statement than right. The naive device in John clearly indicates that he did not emerge from the elite setting of Philo but rather from popular folk echoes of the motifs of the philosophical schools that spilled over into the common mind. The Gospel of John owes no direct debt to Philo, only to the milieu of Philo.

As to Colossians, it is marked by a development uniquely Christian: the progressive deepening of the Christology. One reads in 1:15–20 that Christ is "the image of the invisible God, the first born of all creation; for in him all things were created, in heaven and earth, visible and invisible. . . . In him all the fulness of God was pleased to dwell. . . ." Within the passage, the statement in verse 18 that the Christ is "the head of the body, the church . . . the first born from the dead," obviously has no direct relation to Philonic thought. The passage as a whole, however, is quite reminiscent of Philo.[20] Because there are allusions in 1:23 to the need of the Colossians to "continue in the faith, stable and steadfast," and in 2:8–23 warnings against false teachers and teachings, the passage 1:15–20 is often viewed as presenting the recommended "orthodox view" as a shield against heresies. There has been the effort on the part of scholars to identify the "heretical" views, and here both the documents of Qumran and Philo have been called upon, though perhaps not successfully.

The deepening Christology of unfolding Christianity apparently prompted questions such as, In what way was the Christ like God: partly or completely? And in what way was he human: partly or completely? Respecting the Christ and God, there was apparently a progressive trend towards complete identification, and possibly that is what is intended in the important phrase "fulness of God." In Philo the Logos and the powers never become equated with the *pleroma* ("fulness"). Philo, however, did not have to face the theological issues which arose in Christianity

where the view of the Christ was influenced by event, that is, by
the incarnation of the Christ in the man Jesus. One might say that
important as is the Logos doctrine in Philo, and even central in
his thought, the Logos scarcely is a crux for Philo. Obviously in
unfolding Christian thought the Logos/Christ was indeed such a
crux. Yet out of Philonism one can glimpse the kind of issues that
were destined to lead in later Christianity into diversity and con-
troversy. Philo would scarcely go the distance that the author of
Colossians went in declaring that the Logos/Christ was the *pleroma* of God. Nevertheless, the assertions in Colossians become
clearer with some knowledge of Philo's many statements about
the Logos than they are without that knowledge.[21]

It is the Epistle to the Hebrews that has produced the most frequent assertions of relations between Philonic and developing
Christian thought. Hebrews presents Christianity as the ideal religion, for which Judaism was an imperfect foreshadowing. In a
sense, the usual Philonic contrast between the ideal found in the
intelligible world and its imitation in the sensible world is in Hebrews transformed; Judaism, the "imitation," is chronologically
the precursor; Christianity is chronologically the resultant ideal.
Scholars often speak of the "typology"[22] in Hebrews; Jewish
practices, as in the Tabernacle in the Wilderness, were of the
type that came to perfection in Christianity. One can note that
Philo speaks of the literal Tabernacle and then proceeds to allegorize it, while in Hebrews the imperfect Tabernacle is su-
perseded by the perfect Temple, the "body" of Christ. There
are some analogies, then, between Philonic thought and that
in Hebrews, though the differences in manner need adequate ac-
counting.

C. Spicq[23] described what he considered Philo's great influence
on Hebrews respecting vocabulary, rhetorical devices, and even
themes and structures. Spicq set forth the imaginative possibility
that the author of Hebrews was a former student of Philo, subsequently a convert to Christianity. Accordingly, the author of He-

brews was personally acquainted with Philo's writings. This theory has elicited little acceptance. In general, the scholarship has been willing to accept a general atmospheric accord, or a general Philonic influence, this among others, on Hebrews, but not a specific influence such as Spicq set forth.[24]

Hebrews contains a common Stoic sentiment, found also in Philo, that the sage is a stranger here on earth, for his commonwealth is from heaven. But the perspective is constantly needed that, however little or much Hebrews echoes motifs in Philo, Hebrews is a Christian work. Its main theme is that it is within Christianity that a man is enabled to rise above corporeality through the loving self-sacrifice of the Christ. Hebrews begins with the statement that in the past God had spoken to his people in diverse ways, but recently and climactically he had spoken through a Son.

The Pastoral Epistles (1 and 2 Timothy and Titus) and Epistles like Colossians reflect doctrinal divisions in the church. It is not always possible to identify these. Two second-century "heresies" are often regarded as the principal ones, encratism[25] and docetism.[26] Encratism is excessive self-mortification. When Philo argues for regimenting the senses and passions, he makes it clear that he does not recommend that these be destroyed, for destruction could equal race suicide. Perhaps Philo is opposing encratism, but this is by no means certain. Docetism is the heresy ascribed to gnostics who denied that Jesus had come in the flesh. According to these "heretics," Jesus merely "seemed" to be physical; the root meaning of docetism is "to seem." These two heresies arose out of an extreme dualism and from a contempt for the body and for bodily functions; if Jesus was "real," he was subject to the ingestion, digestion, and egestion of foods. At least one quasi-docetic passage appears in Philo in which he tells[27] that the three angels of Genesis, chapter 18, for whom Abraham had a sumptuous meal prepared, only *seemed* to eat.

Perhaps passingly there are other dim echoes of Philonism elsewhere in the New Testament.[28] It is to be noted that frequently
it is in connection with heresies that passages in Philo are cited.
(Not that Philo is the source of heresies!) In the unfolding of
Christianity, whether on orthodox or heretical lines, the conse-
quences of dualism and the distinction between the sensible and
the intelligible worlds raised the problem of "history," as distinct
from its opposite, which I might here denominate as "existential"
response. That is, Philo's problem with past history is that certain
historical events occurred within the sensible world, but for
Philo these events were of little concern compared with man's
relations with the intelligible world. An extreme but not atypical
example which we have seen is found in his treatment of Sarah
and Hagar at the end of *On Mating*. There Philo asserts that
Scripture has no interest in describing the backyard quarrels of
two women; he goes on there to deny that Sarah and Hagar are
historical persons. Existentially Hagar is the experience of both
Abraham and Philo with the encyclica. Abraham's journey from
Ur to Charran can be of interest to Philo and us only if we too
can make the same spiritual journey, for what difference can it
make to us if one man made a journey a long time ago? True,
Philo usually goes through the process of re-historicizing after he
has de-historicized;[29] but his re-historicizing is consistent, not
with biblical accounts, but with his allegory. Elements in the
Synoptic tradition troubled Clement of Alexandria and Origen,
leading both, but especially Origen, to allegorize such passages. It
is stated in Matt. 11:19 that Jesus came eating and drinking; was
this to be taken as actual history? Was it actual that Jesus was
born, of all places, in Galilee, and was a Jew, and appeared on
earth in Judea, and died under Pontius Pilate? The thin line between orthodoxy and heresy was whether those who preferred an
"existential" approach to Jesus went to the length of denying the
historical. It is to be recalled that in early Christian times, the dis-
putes over Jesus were not the calling into question of his divinity

(as has been done in the past two centuries), but that of his true humanity.

Scholars such as W. Bousset have spoken of a scholastic tradition that moved from Philo to Alexandrian Christians and then to Rome.[30] Modern editions of these Christian writers normally carry cross-references back to Philo, either because the writers directly mention him or else utilize some Philonic idea. As Christian thought developed, it seemed necessary to consult Philo, whether for clarification or for the authority of his name.

Henry Chadwick[31] wrote, "The history of Christian philosophy begins not with a Christian, but with a Jew, Philo of Alexandria. . . . Philo's statements about the Logos were to have a notable future when adopted to the uses of Christian doctrine. . . . We may see some symbolic recognition of the Christian debt to Philo in the legend quoted by Eusebius[32] that when Philo went on his visit to Rome, he met St. Peter."

# Appendix:

## Tools and Current Research

What we might call the standard edition of Philo, with an introduction and critical notes on the text, is the *Editio Major* of Leopold Cohn and Paul Wendland (seven volumes and eight books) (Berlin, 1896–1930). Volume 7 is an index by Hans Leisegang. The *Editio Minor* by Cohen and Wendland is the same as the standard edition, except that there are no notes on the text and there are no prolegomena. The Loeb Classics edition uses the Cohen and Wendland text. From time to time scholars dealing with an individual treatise make their own edition of the text, but for all practical purposes, though, the Cohen-Wendland is today the standard Greek Philo. As for the materials preserved in Armenian, namely, *On Providence* and *On Animals*, and *Questions and Answers to Genesis and Exodus*, these were published and Latin translation given by J. B. Aucher in Venice, in respectively, 1822 and 1826. The 1826 publication includes not only *Questions and Answers to Genesis* and *Questions and Answers to Exodus*, but also three treatises (*On Samson, On Jonah*, and *On God*) which are usually viewed as not authentically by Philo.

The bibliographies of Philo that a student confined to English should be aware of are Erwin R. Goodenough and Howard L. Goodhart, "A General Bibliography of Philo," found in Erwin R. Goodenough, *The Politics of Philo Judeaus* (New Haven, 1938); Louis Feldman, *Studies in Judaica: Scholarship on Philo and Josephus* (1937–1962) (New York, 1963); Earle Hilgert, "A Bibliography of Philo Studies, 1963–1970," *Studia Philonica*, 1 (1972), pp. 57–71; Earle Hilgert, "A Bibliography of Philo Studies, in 1977, with additions for 1965–1970," *Studia Philonica*, 2 (1972), pp. 51–54.

To these may be added two works not in English: Antonio V. Nazzaro, *Recenti Studi Filoniani* (1963–70) (Naples, 1973); Gerhard Delling, *Bibliographie zur jüdisch-hellenistischen und intertestamentarischen Literatur*, 1900–1970 (Berlin, 1975).

Mr. Hilgert has informed me that he has finished a bibliography for the years 1935–1975 which will appear in W. Haase, Editor, *Aufstieg und Niedergang der Römischen Welt*, to be published in Germany, the work being directed from the University of Tübingen. To this same series I contributed an introductory essay on Philo, and Peder Borgen has prepared his "Philo of Alexandria: A Critical and Synthetical Survey of Research since World War II."

There is the recent work by Günther Mayer, *Index Philoneus* (Berlin-New York, 1974), which can be used as a supplement to Leisegang. Unhappily the book gives only the single word being looked up, rather than the passage in which the word occurs, and therefore its utility is somewhat reduced. Professor Peder Borgen of the University of Trondheim in Norway has been nearing completion of his computerized concordance project, and I hear from him that he has progressed to the point where there is at hand a "machine-readable text of Philo's works, including the Greek fragments which are stored on magnetic tape."

The French translation of Philo (*Les Oeuvres de Philon d'Alex-*

*andrie*) under the editorship of Professor Claude Mondesért, being published at Lyons, is moving along. I am informed by Mr. Hilgert that the Greek fragments of *Questions and Answers* was scheduled to appear in the first quarter of 1978. There is awaited early in 1978 a translation of the Armenian texts by Professor Charles Mercier of *Questions and Answers to Genesis*, books 1 and 2; the Latin text of J. B. Aucher was to be reprinted, but the French translation was to be based on the Armenian text. Professor Abraham Terrien of Andrews University in Berrien Springs, Michigan, has nearly completed his work on *De Animalibus*. Mr. Hilgert informs me that Professor Terrien is providing a history of the Armenian texts and a discussion of the peculiar problems of translating classical Armenian versions from the Greek. Professor Terrien will provide an English translation of the treatise, together with an effort to restore the Greek text. Professor Terrien will be reprinting a critical edition of the Armenian text.

As part of the Institute of Antiquity and Christianity at Claremont, California, there is a Philo research project under the direction of Professor Burton Mack. Professor Mack has gathered together an international research team "to investigate biblical exegesis in Alexandrian Judaism. Primary source materials for this investigation are the exegetical writings of Philo. The team will attempt to identify and define the exegetical techniques used by Philo and understand their function in his corpus. This analysis of Philo's reinterpretation of tradition will enable scholars to compare Philo's method with other Jewish, Christian, and Greco-Roman traditions and understand better the environment that produced them." The participating American scholars met together in October, 1977; another meeting is set for 1979. Professor Valentin Nikiprowetzky of Paris attended the October 1977 meeting.

Some of the attention of the Center of Hermeneutical Studies in Berkeley, California (Wilhelm Wuellner is the directing head), frequently has topics on Philo, and these are published. Two scholars associated with the Center, Professors David Winston and John Dillon, are working on a commentary on *De Gigantibus* and *Quod Deus Immutabilis Sit*, with the collaboration of international scholars. Professor James Royse of San Francisco State University has been working on an edition of the fragments of Philo, carrying on the work of the late Ludwig Fruechtel. Let me here record my profound gratitude to Mr. Hilgert for continually keeping me informed of Philonic activities.

Since it is the Greek Bible which is the basis of Philo's interpretation, it is an ordinary procedure to say that Philo used "the Septuagint." However, modern students have become increasingly leery of speaking of the Septuagint, for research has led to a questioning of older views. The Letter of Aristeas, apparently written between 100 and 50 B.C., ascribes the origin of the Greek translation as follows. During the reign of Ptolemy Philadelphus, the eminent librarian Demetrios of Phaleron lamented to the king that the celebrated library, containing the greatest collection of books ever assembled, lacked the Five Books of Moses. The Ptolemy authorized Demetrios to procure a translation. To that end he invited to Alexandria seventy-two priests from Jerusalem who knew Greek as fluently as Hebrew. After a hospitable reception, and a banquet, reminiscent of a Platonic Symposium, the translators set to work and accomplished the objective. (Philo hearkens back to this matter in *On Moses* II; see pp. 51–52). The implication is that the Septuagint (meaning "seventy," a shortening of the actual number of seventy-two) was the result of a deliberate and single incident.

The historical reliability of the tradition found in the Letter of Aristeas has been challenged on two different bases. One has been the allegation that the tradition in the Letter of Aristeas is only a legend, a bit of Jewish apologetics, and is quite incredible. The other basis for challenge has been the assertion that in reality the so-called Septuagint is the end result of a slow process whereby out of a range of earlier, tentative translations, the Septuagint in more or less fixed form slowly emerged. If the Septuagint is the result of a process, then one should more properly speak of early efforts at translation not as *the* Septuagint, but of "Septuagintal types." Consistent with the latter view, it would be more precise to say that the Bible Philo utilized was of a Septuagintal type, rather than "the Septuagint."

There exists, moreover, a complicating factor. In *The Allegory*, as we have said, Philo begins each treatise with a citation of one or more biblical verses. Such a citation is known technically as a *lemma*, plural *lemmata*. Once the citation has been made, Philo proceeds in each treatise to use the words or phrases for his interpretation. It turns out, however, that there are instances in which the quotations in the body of an essay are not identical with what is found in the lemmata. How to explain the divergencies? Peter Katz, in *Philo's Bible: The Aberrant Text of Bible Quotations in Some Philonic Writings and Its Place in the Textual History of the Greek Bible* (Cambridge, 1950), proposed an explanation along the following lines, that medieval copyists tampered with the quotation at the beginning of a treatise to make it conform to the consensus Septuagint, but did not touch the biblical texts in the remainder of the treatise.

There is an additional complexity, at least as some researchers have supposed. The Bible quotations with the treatises that do not conform to the Septuagint have been judged to be closer to the Hebrew text than the Septuagint is in these passages. Two opposite explanations could account for this closer approximation of the Hebrew. One explanation is that the quotations in Philo represent a period before the emergence of a more or less standard Septuagintal text. But an exactly opposite explanation has been suggested, namely, that in the third Christian century, Philo's writings were in some circulation in Caesarea, the Gentile city in Judea. There, under the influence of Jews who were bilingual, alterations were introduced here and there into Philonic manuscripts, deliberately substituting quotations more closely in accord with the Hebrew text for the text as originally cited in Philo. The case for this is made by Dominique Barthélemy, in an essay, "Est-ce Hoshaya Rabbi qui censura le'commentaire allégorique?" in *Philon D'Alexandrie, Lyon, 11–14 Septembre, 1966* (Paris, 1967), pp. 45–78. One might regard this suggestion as more ingenious than convincing.

The matter of Philo's biblical text is a concern more for students of the origin and development of the Septuagint and other Greek versions than it is for Philo and his thought.

# Notes

## Chapter 1

1. *Leg.* 1, 182.
2. He assails Pontius Pilate in *Leg.* 299–305 (see Ch. 3, p. ooo). There is no mention of Jesus in the passage.
3. Philo's writings became useful to Christians in Alexandria. A result was the Christian rewriting of at least one passage, the first part of *Prov.* The view arose that Philo had converted to Christianity; baseless as this is, it nevertheless points to the congruencies between Philo's theological position and that of Christians such as Clement and Origen.
4. A forerunner of Neo-Platonism. He flourished in the latter part of the second Christian century.
5. Wolfson, *Philo*, 2 vols. (Cambridge, Mass., 1947).
6. *Studien zum antiken Synkretismus, aus Iran und Griechenland* (Bonn, 1921), p. 30. See also further such negative assessments in Walther Völker, *Fortschrift und Vollendung bei Philo von Alexandrien* (Leipzig, 1938), p. 44, note 2. Additional disparaging assessments are found gathered in Valentin Nikiprowetzky, *Le Commentaire de l'Ecriture chez Philon d'Alexandrie* (Leiden, 1977), pp. 2–3.
7. *The History of the Jewish People in the Time of Jesus Christ* (Eng. tr.), div. II, vol. 3, p. 330.
8. See S. W. Baron, "Population," *Encyclopedia Judaica*, vol. XIII, pp. 870–71; V. Tcherikover, *Hellenistic Civilization and the Jews*

(Eng. tr.) (Philadelphia, 1959), pp. 286–87. See also Antonio V. Nazzaro, *Recenti Studi Filoniani* (1963–70) (Naples, 1973), p. 73. The passages in Philo which speak of the great abundance of Jews are *Mos.* II, 232 and *Leg.* 32–45.

9. *Leg.* 8; Sukkot 51B. Eminently worth reading is Louis H. Feldman, "The Orthodoxy of the Jews in Hellenistic Egypt," *Jewish Social Studies* XXII (1960): 215–37. The essay deals in great competency with broader matters than its title suggests. On the Jewish partiality for the Ptolemys in the time before Philo, see Arnaldo Momigliano, *Alien Wisdom: The Limits of Hellenization* (Cambridge, 1975), especially pp. 115–20.

10. The granting of isopoliteia is ascribed in *The Jewish War* II, 487–88, to the Diadochoi, the successors to Alexander the Great. In *Antiquities* XII, 8, the grant is ascribed to Ptolemy Soter.

11. *Ant.* XIV, 188.

12. See, in his *Hellenistic Civilization and the Jews*, tr. by S. Applebaum (Philadelphia, 1959), pp. 309–32. He says (p. 309) that on the question of Jewish rights, "Josephus is to be estimated, in the main, not as a historian but as a Jewish apologist. . . ."

13. It was first published in 1926 in H. I. Bell, *Jews and Christians in Egypt*. It is also in Alexander Fuks and Victor Tcherikover, *Corpus Papyrorum Judaicarum*, vol. I, 1953 (Cambridge, Mass., 1957–1964). The scholarly literature on the Rescript is exceedingly abundant, for its content challenges what before its publication had been a usual assumption that the Letter of Claudius was to be taken at face value. Moreover, a passage in the Rescript chides the Jews for their acts of violence; the debate has ensued among scholars whether this violence took place in the year 40 or 41, or as much as a decade later. If the latter, the Rescript would appear to have come from 51. A fine discussion of these complex matters is in Tcherikover, *Ha-Yehudim Be-Mitzraim Bi-Tequfa Ha-Hellenistit-Romit Le-Or Ha-Papyrologia* (place, 1945). A summary is found in the English synopsis of the book on pp. 22–28; it is regrettably brief. See also H. S. Jones, "Claudius and the Jewish Question at Alexandria," *Journal of Roman Studies* XVI (1926): 17–35.

On the matter of Jewish uprisings, the documents and attendant scholarship respecting the "Alexandrian martyrs" are of some utility. Friction between Jews and Egyptians seem to have been frequent, with both communities eager for the higher status which

Greeks enjoyed; apparently the two communities took out their frustrations on each other. Philo repeatedly scorns the Egyptians mentioned in the accounts of Abraham and Joseph, but means the Egyptians of his times. As to the Alexandrian "martyrs," some Alexandrian anti-Semites were executed in Rome by the Emperor. Scattered third century papyri hearken back to these events; some of the papyri restrict their blaming to the Romans, but a few state that the men who died were victims of a joint Roman-Jewish conspiracy. The lateness of the papyri, and their tendentiousness, have aroused scholarly skepticism. An excellent analysis is in Tcherikover, pp. 158–71. Tcherikover brings these matters to bear on the dating of the Rescript; he accepts 41.

14. *Hellenistic Civilization and the Jews*, Eng. tr., p. 306. Tcherikover is of the opinion that the single known "trace of the exemption of the Jews from the worship of the divine Caesar" had a "special reason connected with contemporary events."

15. The latter quotation is from Strabo, quoted in *Antiquities* XIX, 117. The source of the former is the Talmud, Sukkot 51B, and Tosephta Sukkot IV, 6.

16. Josephus uses it in *Ant.* XVIII, 159–60; XIX, 276; XX, 100, 147, and *Wars* V, 205.

17. Tensions before Philo's time are reflected in III Maccabees; those after are narrated by Josephus, *War* II: 487.

18. This thesis is fully developed in *The Jurisprudence of the Jewish Courts in Egypt* (New Haven, 1929). The thesis is virtually everywhere rejected; see Tcherikover, *Ha-Yehudim*, pp. 138–39, note 25. Tcherikover is especially critical of Goodenough's view (pp. 33 ff.) that Jewish courts possessed the right of lynching.

19. *Spec.* III, 1 ff.

20. See his "Philo and Public Life," *Journal of Egyptian Archeology* XII (1926): 77–79. J. Schwartz in two writings, "Note sur la famille de Philon d'Alexandrie," *Annuaire de l'Institut de Philologie et d'Histoire Orientales et Slaves de l'Université de Bruxelle* XIII (1953): 591–602, and "L'Egypte de Philon," in *Philon d'Alexandrie, Lyons, 1966* (Paris, 1967), reconstructs a bit too freely the family connections of Philo. His work is criticized in the as yet unpublished Ph.D. dissertation by S. Stephen Foster, "The Alexandrian Situation and Philo's Use of *Dike*."

21. In *Leg.* 370 the deputation numbers five; Josephus *Ant.* speaks of a three-man deputation.

22. See my *Judaism and Christian Beginnings* (New York, 1978), pp. 262–65.

23. He is listed in encyclopedias under Alexander, Tiberius. I have not succeeded in obtaining A. Lepape, "Tiberius Julius Alexander, Prefet d' Alexandrie et de L'Egypte," *Bulletin de la Societé royale d'Archeologie d'Alexandrie*, n.s. VIII (1934): 331–41. See p. 63 on Joseph as a cryptic figure for this nephew.

24. The awareness by Jews of Philo begins with Azariah de Rossi, a Venetian Rabbi, in his Hebrew work, *Meor Enayaim*. De Rossi was a product of the Renaissance. See Ralph Marcus, "A 16th Century Hebrew Critique of Philo," *Hebrew Union College Annual* XXI (1948): 29–69.

## Chapter 2

1. *Abr.* 66; *QGI* 17.

2. This allegory is found in Plutarch, *De Liberis Educandis*. F. H. Colson, "Philo on Education," *Journal of Theological Studies* XVIII (1917): 153–54 mentions other extant versions of the broadly known allegory. See also Wolfson I, pp. 145–46, and H. Von Arnim, *Stoicorum Veterum Fragmenta*, I, p. 78.

3. As we shall see below, true wisdom equals generic virtue, and, in effect, true religion, which in effect is Judaism. Different as these may seem, they are synonymous for Philo.

4. See "Allegorical Interpretation," *Jewish Encyclopedia*, vol. I, pp. 403–7. The Hebrew terms are *dorshe r'shumot* and *dorshe hamurot*.

5. I have not been readily able to obtain Karl Staehle, *Die Zahlenmystik bei Philon von Alexandereia* (place, 1931). I read it some thirty years ago, at a time when for about six months I was preoccupied with inquiring into Philo's numbers, a tedious chore I felt compelled to try to master. Alas, one can often readily forget what one has read!

6. See note 4 above.

## Chapter 3

1. Ordinarily scholars accept, though with occasional disagreement, the arrangement of M. L. Massebieau, *Le Classement des Oeuvres de Philon*, Bibliotheque de l'Ecole des Haute Etudes . . . Science religieuses, I (Paris, 1889), pp. 1–91.

2. A brief but adequate discussion of the meaning of the word is given by F. H. Colson, LCL Philo VII, pp. 407–13.

3. *Preparation for the Gospel,* VIII, 6:1–9 and VIII, 11:1–18.

4. See note 2.

5. Philo speaks of people who have abused Moses "as an imposter and prating mountebank." Josephus, too, in his *Against Apion* (for example, II, 145) feels the need to defend the character of Moses against detractors.

6. Josephus in *Against Apion* II also treats the Mosaic Laws as the "constitution" of the Jews. A good bit of the material here in Philo appears also in *Against Apion* II, there also treated as elements in the "constitution." I see no direct literary connection between Philo and Josephus.

7. F. H. Colson (LCL Philo IX, pp. 514–15) gives a digest of what Philo tells about the Essenes as a prelude to comparing this with what Josephus tells about them (primarily in *Jewish War* II, 119–59 and *Antiquities* XVIII, 18–22). While Colson in his note specifies what Josephus contains but which is lacking in Philo, he abstains from noting some acute differences within what they present in common.

8. F. H. Colson (LCL Philo IX, pp. 515–16) conjectures that Philo is alluding to Herod the Great, whom Josephus in *Ant.* XV, 372, describes as treating the Essenes with special friendship, regarding them as higher than other mortals.

9. This is mentioned in the second fragment (*Providence* 2:64) in Eusebius (see note 3 above), *Preparation for the Gospel* VIII, 14.

10. On the subtitle, see below, p. 69.

11. *Jewish War* II, 160–61.

12. *Die Therapeuten und ihre Stellung in der Geschichte der Askese: Eine kritische Untersuchung der Schrift: De vita contemplativa* (Strassburg, 1880).

13. In Sandmel, pp. 194–96, I recorded the various overlaps in Philo's allegorical treatment of Abraham with his treatment of the Therapeutae.

14. *Ant.* XVIII, *Jewish War* II, 119–66.

15. I think that Colson LCL, IX, p. 106, note a, is right in supposing that Philo is alluding not to *Every Good Man Is Free* or to the *Hypothetica,* but to a third composition on the Essenes which has been lost.

16. The phrase is from Plato. As we shall see, neither *theos* ("God")

nor *kyrios* ("lord"), biblical terms connote God Himself, but only aspects—Philo calls them "powers"—of God. See below, p. 92.

17. Philo uses figures of speech. For example, those who have the vision of God "are carried away by a heaven sent passion of love, remain rapt and possessed like bacchanals or corybants. . . ."

18. Philo, either through carelessness or through scribal error, seems to be saying that the assemblies take place "after seven sets of seven days. . . . This is the eve of the chief feast which takes Fifty for its own." The latter allusion on the surface seems to be to Pentecost, but it is surprising for Pentecost to be called "the chief feast." Colson, LCL IX, pp. 152 and 522–23, seems to rule out the possibility of a departure from the Mosaic calendar, but he wrote before the discovery of the Dead Sea Scrolls which, like Jubilees, use an "unorthodox" calendar, possibly what is called the "pentecontad," in which a year consisted of seven periods of 50 days, with two interstitial periods, one of eight days and one of seven, to bring the count of days to 365.

19. It is to be recalled that at ancient banquets, one did not sit, but instead reclined on couches. In the inherited traditional Passover seder, one of the four questions, asked by the youngest person present, is this: "On all nights, we either sit or recline; on this night, all of us recline." In some traditional homes the "reclining" is commemorated by a pillow placed at the back of the chair of the father.

20. The Greek word is *nous*. Colson notes that *nous* can mean either "mind" or "meaning" and that "Philo hardly distinguishes the two."

21. Philo writes that Flaccus *also* underwent a miserable outcome. The word *also*, plus an allusion in *Leg.* 160, leads to the view that this treatise was the second of two, the first being about the misdeeds of Sejanus.

22. Philo does not identify "the host." From a passage in Josephus, *Ant.* XIX, 276–77, it is likely that the host was Philo's brother. The purpose of the call was to get some funds, and the purpose was finally achieved; *Ant.* XVIII, 159–60.

23. Philo singles out the instance of a certain lunatic named Carabas, whom a mob dressed in robes and hailed as *Marin* ("Lord" in Aramaic), thus pouring scorn on Agrippa. It is to be recalled that the language in Judea had shifted centuries before from Hebrew to Aramaic.

24. LCL, IX, p. 301.

25. A note, LCL, X, p. vii, dated in November 1943, speaks of Colson's death but does not tell when it occurred.

26. In "Philo's Exposition of the Law and His De Vita Mosis," *Harvard Theological Review* 27 (1933): 109–25.

27. Philo chides Greek men of letters for ignoring Moses; he charges them with writing "comedies and pieces of voluptuous license," rather than choosing to provide "lessons taught by good men. . . ."

28. In Jewish lore, the term for the embellishment of Scripture, originally conveyed orally, is *haggada;* see p. 128. Philo tells that Moses from birth "had an appearance of more than ordinary goodliness"; this is not found in Scripture and hence is to be classified as within *haggda.*

29. It can be useful to a student to compare, for example, Exod. 1:1–4:17 with *Mos.* 5–84.

30. On the characteristics of biblical narrative, see my *The Enjoyment of Scripture* (New York, 1972), pp. 15–17.

31. See *The Republic* V, 473 D.

32. See Exod. 34:30–35.

33. In Greek, *physis*. See p. 120.

34. Other minor deviations are present. Philo does not mention the number of the translators; he tells that the king-high priest of Judea selected the translators; he alters the "symposium."

35. The Greek is *enthousiōntes*.

36. The translation is Colson's. The English of "priests and prophets of the mysteries" is in Greek *hierophantas kai prophetas*. That is, the words "of the mysteries" are not in the Greek, but derive, as Colson knew, from the usual meaning of hierophant.

37. George Howard, "The Letter of Aristeas and Diaspora Judaism," *Journal of Theological Studies* (new series) XXII (1971): 337–48, suggests that the purpose of the Letter of Aristeas is an apology directed to Judea, justifying Alexandrian Jews as loyal and worthy. It is not, according to Howard, an apology addressed to the Gentile world.

38. Perhaps my view here is influenced by modern American circumstances. The theme is readily found in parochial Jewish apologetics that so highly do American Gentiles laud Judaism that half-assimilated American Jews should do so also. Such views are both implicit and explicit in articles and books on the "Jewish contribution" to modern civilization.

39. In the usual arrangement of Philo's treatises, *On the Creation* is found in the first position. Next come the treatises in *The Allegory*. Thus, in the LCL edition, *On Creation*, part of *The Exposition*, is in volume one, and the next treatise in *The Exposition* found in volume six.

40. See Wisdom of Solomon 11:17 which seems to assert that God made the world out of matter without form." Philo seems to be rejecting this view.

41. The allusion is to the Greek and Egyptian myths about the gods.

42. Philo, as it were, distinguishes between the "first man," the ideal, spiritual man, and Adam, a material copy of the first man. Adam in Philo's allegory is the mind, neither a gifted nor deficient mind, but simply a mind in general.

43. Generic virtue exists in the *kosmos noetos*, there being the idea of virtue. The cardinal virtues, as presented by the Stoics, number four; justice, bravery, prudence, and moderation, exist in the *kosmos aesthetikos*, since we all know men who possess one or more of the four.

44. Goodenough, pp. 43–44, terms this set of five points as "the first creed of history." Perhaps. But at least in the Christian sense a creed was an authoritative statement which had or came to have an obligatory aspect. I doubt that creed is a felicitous term to describe these five points.

45. On the variant readings and the implications, see my "Genesis 4:26B," *Two Living Traditions* (Detroit, 1972), pp. 305–15. Briefly, the verse in the Hebrew seems to ascribe the first awareness of the existence of God to Enos, whereas in the Jewish tradition that achievement was Abraham's. Jewish exegesis, in the Targumim ("Aramaic translations") and the Septuagint, render the verse against its normal meaning so as to preserve the achievement for Abraham.

46. Gen. 5:24 reads a bit differently in the Septuagint than in the Hebrew, substituting "well-pleasing to God" for the Hebrew "walked with God"; "he has not found" replaces the Hebrew, "he was not"; "translated him" replaces "took him."

47. These are basically Aristotelian; see Sandmel, p. 106, for further details.

48. See Philo's transition in 208.

49. It is also used in Fourth Maccabees.

50. The text tells that Abraham, Isaac, and two servants "*arrived* on

the third day at the *place* about which God had spoken to him. On the third day, Abraham raised his eyes and saw the place from the distance." What is the *place* which a man can arrive at and yet remain distant? The answer is God. *Place* is a synonym for God. So too in Rabbinic literature, *Ha-Maqom*, "the place," is an epithet for God.

51. This is an embellishment, absent from Scripture.

52. Elsewhere the Scriptural prophets are God's "family" (*On Dreams* I, 193–95; see Sandmel, p. 177, especially note 347).

53. The Septuagint here reads a bit differently from the Hebrew.

54. I assembled this abundance in *Philo's Place in Judaism: A Study of Conceptions of Abraham in Jewish Literature* (New York, 1971), pp. 141–85. The chapter on Abraham in Goodenough, *BLL,* was based solely on *On Abraham;* it is therefore incomplete, and the incompleteness led Goodenough to some errors, e.g., his statement that Philo does not mention Melchizedek.

55. The name "Joseph" in Hebrew, according to Philo, means "addition of a lord."

56. See my "The Confrontation of Greek and Jewish Ethics: Philo, *De Decalogo,*" in *Two Living Traditions* (Detroit, 1972), pp. 279–90.

57. In *On the Decalogue* 154–75 are in effect an epitome of *On the Special Laws,* Books II, III, and IV, 1–131.

58. On the deviations in enumeration, both those of Philo and Josephus, and also the traditional Christian from the Jewish, see "Decalogue," *Jewish Encyclopedia,* vol. IV, pp. 492–96, and there "Sequence and Numbering," pp. 495–96.

59. See my "Virtue and Reward in Philo," *Essays in Old Testament Ethics,* James L. Crenshaw and John T. Willis, eds. (New York, 1974).

60. Whether this is an allusion specifically to his participation in the deputation to Gaius Caligula, as most scholars infer, or to less spectacular involvements, is uncertain. In *Somni* II, 123–32, Philo alludes to a prefect who "purposed to disturb our ancestral customs and especially to do away with the law" of the Sabbath, this as a prelude to "irregularity in all other matters, and a general backsliding." The historical allusion here does not seem to be to Flaccus; unhappily it is scarcely to be known to what it refers. Later, in *Spec. Leg.* III (159–68), Philo mentions an episode of oppression by a tax-collector who abducted the families of debtors who, unable to

pay the assessments, took to flight; the tax-collector executed those whom he had abducted. But Philo does not tell us when this happened or who the tax-collector was.

61. *On the Virtues*, as we have inherited it, begins with Philo's statement that he has already discussed justice and will now move on to courage.

62. See LCL, VIII, pp. XII ff., and the note on p. 440, respecting the title of the treatise.

63. Colson translates the sub-title *philanthropeia* as "humanity," recognizing its inadequacy. Were it not that "philanthropy" in our time has come to be a synonym for charity to the poor, philanthropy would be a better term. At times "humaneness" is a good rendering, but at times it is inadequate.

64. The Midianites, through women, tried to seduce the Hebrews away from God (Num. 25:1–16; 31:9–17); the Moabite king here is Balak, who hired Balaam to curse the Hebrews (Num. 22:2ff.)

65. See Colson, LCL, VIII, pp. 437–39, and above, pp. 85 and 104. Philo does not mean by democracy what we mean, but a situation in which a philosopher-king has all parts and aspects of his domain in proper relationship.

66. Colson's translation is ambiguous and seems to represent a slip (205); he has Adam exchanging "mortality for immortality"; Philo's intent is that Adam abandoned immortality and went to mortality. I think Colson's words can be defended, but in this rare instance his customary full clarity is missing.

67. See Genesis, chapter 25, especially vv. 5–6; there Abraham "sends away" the children born to him by Keturah.

68. One wonders why Philo here reverts to Abraham, whom he wrote about similarly in *On Abraham*. Possibly *On the Virtues* is a separate writing which ought not be classified with *The Exposition*.

69. See my "Abraham's Knowledge of the Existence of God," *Harvard Theological Review* 44 (1951): 137–39, and its citation of W. L. Knox, "Abraham and the Quest for God" (*HTR* 28 (1935): 55–60).

70. Philo provides detail about Tamar not found in Scripture.

71. This identification is apparently unique to Philo. It is the sort of legendary embellishment found in Cleodemus-Malchus who tells that Abraham's sons by Keturah went to Libya with Hercules; a granddaughter married Hercules; see my *Judaism and Christian Beginnings* (New York, 1978), pp. 264 and 463, note 16. Somewhat

similarly (in *Somni* I, 58) Philo identifies Terah, the father of Abraham, with Socrates.

72. By "ill-sounding" Philo apparently has in mind Gen. 32:5 in the Septuagint. That verse, following after Jacob's wrestling with the angel, speaks of the injury to his thigh; 32:5 LXX reads that "the broad part of the thigh was numbed"; the latter, allegorically, suggest arrogance and pride. "Broad part of the thigh" may have seemed ill-sounding.

73. See LCL, VIII, p. 360, footnote 1.

74. For example, Deuteronomy, chapter 28; Lev. 29:7; 28:1,7; and Deut. 30:11–14.

75. The precise allusion is unclear. In the Palestinian tradition the ninth of Ab, a fast day, commemorated the destruction of the Temple in 587 B.C. (and that in A.D. 70).

76. Carl Siegfried, *Philo von Alexandria als Ausleger des Alten Testaments* (Jena, 1875). The article, "Philo Judaeus," *Jewish Encyclopedia*, vol. X, pp. 6–15, is by Siegfried.

77. Emile Bréhier, *Les idées philosophiques et religieuses de Philon d'Alexandrie*, 2nd ed., Paris, 1925.

78. James Drummond, *Philo Judaeus; or, the Jewish-Alexandrian Philosophy in its Development and Completion*, 2 vols. (London, 1888); reprinted, Amsterdam, 1969.

79. See preceding note. Yonge in vol. 4 translates only the first three books of *Questions and Answers to Genesis*.

80. *The Essential Philo*, Nahum Glatzer, ed. (New York, 1971), uses the translation by C. D. Yonge, *The Works of Philo Judaeus* (Bohn's Ecclesiastical Library), 4 vols. (London, 1854–1865). The notes by Glatzer are scant and of remarkably little helpfulness.

81. These are printed without translation as Appendix A in LCL Supplement II, pp. 179–263. Appendix B (pp. 269–75) reprints additions found in Old Latin.

82. Ralph Marcus, *LCL* Supplement I, p. x, note a, states that *Questions* is later, this on the basis of occasional references there to the *Allegory;* he cites *QE* II, 4 and II, 34, 113. I do not see the aptness of the citation of *QE* II, 113. The view of Schuerer, *Geschichte des jüdische Volkes*[3], vol. 3, p. 501, is that *Questions* is in part earlier, in part later.

# Chapter 4

1. For example, as between salvation mediated by the Church and salvation solely through Scripture.

2. Especially Protestant churches which do not have rich and repeated liturgical practices.

3. See Ch. 9, "Philo and Palestinian Judaism."

4. See LXX Gen. 4:26. See my "Genesis 4:26B," *Hebrew Union College Annual* XXXII (1961), and *Two Living Traditions* (Detroit, 1972), pp. 305–15.

5. Goodenough (*By Light, Light*, pp. 96) says that for convenience he will speak of the lower as the "mystery of Aaron" and of the higher as the "mystery of Moses"; thereafter he uses these terms with great frequency. Let it be noted that "mystery of Aaron" and "mystery of Moses" are Goodenough's terms; the terms have entered into some of the secondary literature, as if they are Philo's terms; they are not. See below, p. 143.

# Chapter 5

1. See Wolfson I, p. 211. The Philonic passages are *Spec.* I, 5, 30; *Spec.* II, 32, 198; *Apif.* 24, 74; *Somni* I, 11, 67; *Conf.* 38, 196.

2. Wolfson, *Philo* (Cambridge, 1947), vol. 1, p. 211.

3. *L.A.*, I, 44.

4. *Decal.* 81; *Spec.* II, 53.

5. The Stoic terms are *logos prophorikos*, uttered speech, and *logos endiathetos*, in unuttered speech or thought.

6. This is based on Exod. 4:10–16, wherein the Deity designates Aaron as the mouth for Moses.

7. By *true* philosophy, Philo means Judaism. He is ambivalent toward the schools of Greek philosophy, at times praising them, but more usually scorning them as dispensable sophistry. The availability in Alexandria of countless public lectures on philosophy moves Philo to dismiss them as sheer wastes of time, since those in attendance at them are in effect deaf to what they hear; true philosophy brings about an effect in conduct by its devotees (*Cong.* 64–68). He defines philosophy in Stoic terms (*Cong.* 79) as "the practice or study of wisdom, and wisdom is the knowledge of things divine and human and their causes."

8. The text in the Septuagint reads "guarded"; Philo in one passage (*Mig.* 130) quotes as if it read "did" (*epoiēse* in place of *ephulaxe*).

9. *Mig.* 130.

10. Philo speaks of them as the "first" in creation, but first is not related to time as much as to priority in significance; Wolfson I, pp. 206–17.

11. See Wolfson I, p. 217.

12. This is based on the interpretation of Gen. 15:10; Philo holds that God there does the cutting. See *Heres* 130 ff.

13. In terms of some aspects of modern psychology, the *elenchos* is analagous to the "super-ego," which can blunt or complete the drive contained in the "id."

# Chapter 6

1. Wolfson II, p. 333. The mentions of David are *Conf.* 28, 149; *Plant.* 81; *Agr.* 9, 12, 39, 50. Solomon is mentioned a single time, but as the author of Proverbs, not as the king, *Cong.* 177.

2. Wolfson II, pp. 323–24. But Wolfson also attempts to make a case (p. 324) for Philo's drawing on "certain oral Jewish tradition." What he presents in this latter regard can seem to be very strained.

3. See Erwin R. Goodenough, "The Political Philosophy of Hellenistic Kingship," *Yale Classical Studies* 1 (1928): 55–102, and his *The Politics of Philo Judaeus, Practice and Theory* (New Haven, 1938).

4. The Masoretic text reads *nasi'* which is usually rendered prince; the Septuagint word here is *basileus*.

5. *Spec. Laws* IV, 29, 151–56.

6. *Mut.* 28, 151.

7. *Spec. Laws* IV, 30, 157.

8. *Mut.* 28, 141–52.

9. *Rewards* 9, 54.

10. It does not seem to me that Wayne A. Meeks, "Moses as God and King," *Religions in Antiquity* (Leiden, 1968), pp. 354–71, adequately notices the margin of difference between what in English would be a "God-like man," and a man as literally divine. I cannot subscribe to the view that Moses is regarded literally as a god in the passages cited in this essay.

11. See Wolfson II, p. 331, and there note 69.

12. This was the Grand Sanhedrin. Local cities had a smaller Sanhedrin of twenty-three.

13. Wolfson II, p. 350.

14. Wolfson II, p. 356; *Spec.* I, 9, 51; *Virt.* 20, 102.

15. *Spec.* I, 9, 52; *Virt.* 20, 103.

16. Philo cites in *Leg.* 30, 200–201 as an example Gentiles who dwelled in the Judean city Jamnia. He denounces them for the injury they have done in violating Jewish sensibilities during the reign of Gaius Caligula.

17. *Flacc.* 7, 48–49.

18. *Confus.* 2, *QGI* 53, III, 43, IV, 168.

19. While Wolfson's discussion (I, pp. 82–85) seems unsatisfying because he cites no strong supporting evidence, it is worth reading.

20. Philo so treats the account of Abraham that the patriarch, having come to the knowledge of the existence of God, this by his migration to Harran, then made a second migration, this to the Wilderness. The basis for the latter is LXX Gen. 12:9; where the Hebrew reads *ha-negbāh* ("southward"), but LXX reads *erema* ("Wilderness").

21. "Alien" is perhaps too strong. Philo says that the Dispersion Jews are colonies of the Jewish population of Judea, but regard the cities of their birth as their *patris*, as Jerusalem is of Jews born therein. Judean and Dispersion Jews together constitute the corporate Israel.

22. *Moses* II, 51, 288.

23. *Praem.* 28–29.

24. *Ibid.*, 29, 165, based on Deut. 30:5.

25. *Ibid.*, 91 ff. (The references in Wolfson II, p. 409, note 57, are garbled.)

26. *Ibid.*, 171.

27. *Moses* II, 44.

## Chapter 7

1. The issue of theodicy, of great importance in itself, is not relevant to the discussion here. On theodicy see my *The Hebrew Scriptures: An Introduction to Their Literature and Religious Ideas* (New York, 1978), pp. 122–23.

2. For a convenient summary on the evil yetzer, see my *Judaism and Christian Beginnings* (New York, 1978), pp. 179–80. Whether

*yetzer* is adequately rendered in English by "impulse" is question-able, but I know of no better rendering.

3. *L. A.* I, 57.

4. See, for example, *Cher.* 3–10 and *Mut.* 77–79.

5. *Cher.* 50.

6. *Spec.* II, 54–55.

7. *L. A.* II, 82; *Cher.* 9–10; *Congr.* 9, 13, 79–80; *Mut.* 79.

8. Repeatedly in *Cong.*, e.g., 79.

9. See pp. 113–14.

10. *Cher.* 45–52.

11. *L. A.* III, 217; *Post.* 134; *Ebr.* 59; *Deter.* 124. See Sandmel, p. 174, note 340.

12. *Abr.* 200–204; *L. A.* III, 209. See Sandmel, pp. 175–76, and note 342.

13. *Plant.* 126–29; *Cher.* 99–100, which seems to view temples as un-necessary.

14. *Spec.* I, 272.

15. Wolfson II, pp. 268–79.

16. *Ibid.*, II, p. 296.

17. In a number of passages, Philo speaks of Hades (*Cong.* 57; *Heres* 45; *Somni* I, 151), but seems to regard it not as connected with the afterlife but as a life of damnation and guilt in this world; see Wolfson I, p. 412.

18. *QG* III, 11.

19. *Heres* 280.

20. *QG* III, 11.

21. *Sacri.* 5.

## Chapter 8

1. In "Nomos Physeos: The Concept of Natural Law in Greek Thought," *Religions in Antiquity*, Jacob Neusner, ed. (Leiden, 1968), pp. 521–41. The quotation is found on p. 522. In the article, Koester gives a survey of the pre-Philonic use of the phrase, show-ing the infrequency of its occurrence.

2. See *Moses* II, 13–14. There Philo contrasts usual human laws with those of Moses "which stand firm, unshaken . . . stamped with the seals of nature herself."

3. Koester, *op. cit.*, p. 531: "In Philo, the Aristotelian conception of the *natura creatrix*"—nature the creator—"was combined with the Jewish belief in the Creator God."

4. Koester (*op. cit.*, p. 536), contends that Philo is here dealing with a Platonic, not a Stoic structure.

5. "L'exégèse de Philon d'Alexandrie," *Revue d'Histoire et de Philosophie Religieuses* (Lille, 1973), pp. 309–29, especially p. 328. Nikiprowetzky stresses that Philo never neglects the literal sense of Scripture in either a systematic or capricious sense. Nikiprowetzky opposes an older view which had suggested that there was a development in Philo's thought, this from an original concern with the literal and later with the allegorical. Nikiprowetzky's essay is extremely perceptive and valuable, one which no advanced student can neglect.

6. In the French translation series, vol. 15. *Quis Rerum Divinarum Sit.* Professor Harl's introductory essay is extraordinarily perceptive.

7. See Goodenough, pp. 16 ff., and his citation of Walther Völker, *Fortschritt und Vollendung bei Philo von Alexandrien* (Leipzig, 1938), who restricts mysticism to Christianity: "There exists no true mysticism apart from *en Christō* and the sacrament."

## Chapter 9

1. See Bernard Bamberger, "The Dating of Aggadic Materials," *Journal of Biblical Literature* LXVIII (1949): 115–23. Bamberger stresses the presence of ancient materials in later collections. Moreover, the circumstance that some haggadic item is specifically ascribed to a sage who flourished in a later time, does not mean that that item is not earlier than that particular sage—a view that is demonstrably right. But Bamberger does not present a "fool-proof" method whereby the dating of materials can be assured.

2. See the preceding note. Bamberger notes the presence of haggadic items in Jubilees, Josephus, and the Rabbis.

3. Josephus in *Antiquities*, in his recasting of Scripture, presents haggadic and halachic innovations. Josephus was born about 37; that is, his lifetime overlapped briefly that of Philo. It could be presumed that haggadic and halachic materials available to Josephus were likewise available to Philo. The best study of these materials on Josephus is Solomon Rappaport, *Agada und Exegese bei Flavius Josephus* (Vienna, 1930).

4. The first published list is found in Adolf Deissmann, *Veröffentlichungen aus der Heidelberger Papyrus-Sammlung*, I (Heidelberg,

1905), pp. 86–93. A subsequently discovered list was published by
D. Rokeah in *Journal of Theological Studies* XIX (1968): 70–82.

5. There are vague echoes of communication, ranging from the two
letters in II Maccabees, written from Judea to Egyptian Jews
through the occasional mentions of Alexandria or Alexandrians in
Rabbinic literature.

6. The scholarship reflects a range of views: one, Philo was independent of Judea; two, Philo in part was dependent and in part
independent; three, Philo was a source for Judean dependence on
him. See Sandmel, pp. 9–26, for details.

7. *Philo und die Halacha. Eine vergleichende Studie unter steter
Berücksichtigung des Josephus* (Leipzig, 1879).

8. *The Alexandrian Halakha in Apologetic Literature of the First
Century C.E.* (Philadelphia, 1936); *Philo and the Oral Law* (Cam-
bridge, 1940); and a Hebrew work, whose title in translation is
*The Midrash Questions and Answers to Genesis and Exodus of
Philo of Alexandria and Its Relation to the Palestinian Midrash*
(New York, 1960); the back cover of this book gives the title as
*Philo's Quaestiones et Solutiones on Genesis and Exodus: The
oldest recorded [sic!] Palestintian Midrash.* In the latter volume
Belkin alludes to some of his essays published in Hebrew pe-
riodicals.

9. "La halacha de Philon selon le premier livre des lois spéciales,"
*Philon D'Alexandrie: Lyon, 11–15 Septembre 1966* (Paris, 1967),
pp. 221–40. Madame Daniel seems to me to beg the basic question,
for she deliberately by-passes the issue of the exegetical methods
by which the supposed halachic similarities are arrived at. In my
judgment the method is more crucial than the accident of halachic
similarity. Madame Daniel goes on to suggest that not only
did Philo know Hebrew quite thoroughly, but that he prepared
his own translation of Scripture from Hebrew into Greek. One has
the feeling that this is all a bit far-fetched. In the discussion following Madame Daniel's paper (p. 241), Dominique Barthélemy asserted that Philo was a halachist but that he did not know Hebrew.
Another discussant, Madame Starobinski, suggested that there were
various levels of the knowledge of Hebrew and that Philo was able
to refer to the Hebrew but he did not really possess a knowledge
of it.

10. In his *Philons griechische und jüdische Bildung*[2] (Darmstadt, 1962).
The issue of whether or not Hellenistic Judaism was significantly

different from Palestinian is complex. The Greek presence in Judea suggests Greek influence on the Judaism there. Greek words in abundance are preserved in Rabbinic literature; so too are echoes, vague and indistinct, of Greek philosophical ideas (see Morton Smith, "The Image of God: Notes on the Hellenization of Judaism . . . ," *Bulletin of the John Rylands Library* XL [1958]: 473–512). But were Palestinian Jews by and large profoundly Hellenized there? A recent view, Martin Hengel, *Judaism and Hellenism*, tr. by J. Bowden, 2 vols. (Philadelphia, 1974), holds that all of Judean thought and literature was profoundly influenced and that we must cease to differentiate between Palestinian and Hellenistic Judaism. Several of us have been critical of Hengel; I wrote that his view is both an overstatement and an invitation to semantic confusion (*Journal of Ecumenical Studies* XI, No. 4, Fall, 1974). A full critique, indeed in effect a refutation, is found in Louis H. Feldman, "Hengel's *Judaism and Hellenism* in Retrospect," *Journal of Biblical Literature* XCVI (1977): 371–82.

11. In my "Parallelomania," *Two Living Traditions* (Detroit, 1972), pp. 291–304, and *Journal of Biblical Literature* LXXXI (1962): 1–13, I presented some reservations respecting a tendency among scholars to exaggerate such overlap, and to make conclusions which frequently consider as identical statements those that are quite diverse in import. In my judgment, Wolfson trespasses in such regards with great frequency.

12. For example, Wolfson I, pp. 188–93, equates the "unwritten law of nature" of Philo with the "oral Torah" of Rabbinic tradition. His effort to refute Isaak Heinemann, "Die Lehre vom ungeschriebenen Gesetz in jüdischen Schrifttum," *Hebrew Union College Annual* IV (1927): 149–71, is quite unsuccessful.

# Chapter 10

1. The conference papers were published in *Le Origine dello Gnosticismo* (Leiden, 1967).
2. *Le Origine*, pp. xx–xxxii.
3. In his "Reply," in J. Philip Hyatt, *The Bible in Modern Scholarship* (New York, 1965), pp. 279–93; the quotation is found on p. 293.
4. In Goodenough *BLL*, p. 119. See the Introduction to the Ktav reprint of Sandmel, 1971, pp. xvii–xviii.

5. See Sandmel, pp. xix–xx, for the citation of Marcel Simon. Henry Chadwick, "St. Paul and Philo of Alexandria," *Bulletin of the John Rylands Library* XLVIII (1965–66): 305 and footnote 5 there gives a very good list of Philonic passages which prove what Chadwick calls "anticipations of second-century gnosticism."

6. Walter Schmithal, *Die Gnosis in Korinth* (Göttingen, 1956), and Robert Jewett, "The Agitators and the Galatian Congregation," *New Testament Studies* XVII (1970): 198–212.

## Chapter 11

1. The great scholar of Tübingen, F. C. Baur, treated the issue of the rapid Hellenization of Christianity by denying that it had taken place. His view was that most of the literature of the New Testament was composed in the second Christian century; most of the Epistles of Paul were second-century writings which falsely ascribed to Paul the authorship of Epistles written at least a century after his time. If so, there was no rapid Hellenization. I do not recall any attention by Goodenough to the Baur theory.

2. See Goodenough, pp. 184–207.

3. Goodenough *BLL*, pp. 11–14, 14–23.

4. *Cher.* 43–50; *Mut.* 137–41; *L.A.* III, 219; *Deter.* 124; see also Sandmel, pp. 174–75 and notes 340–41.

5. See Wilfred L. Knox, *St. Paul and the Church of the Gentiles* (Cambridge, 1939), pp. 29–30. Knox wrote (p. 29): "With a rather bold extension of [Hellenistic Jewish] exegesis it was possible to assimilate Judaism to a mystery-cult to a remarkable extent." In his preface (p. ix), Knox wrote: "Professor E. R. Goodenough's *By Light, Light* did not come into my hands until this book had almost reached its final shape. . . . I am quite clear that his attempt to read a 'Light-mystery' religion into Philo's writings entirely misconceives the whole aim of Philo's work. He writes of the 'passionate desire of the Hellenistic man to experience emotionally the concepts he has learned from Greek rationalism.' The opposite seems to me to be the case; the passionate desire of the Hellenistic man . . . was to find a philosophic basis which would justify him in continuing to practice the form of religion which attracted him or which he inherited. . . ."

6. See Goodenough, pp. 27–28. His essay, "Religionswissenschaft," was published in the American Council of Learned Societies News-

letter X (1959): 5–19. It was reprinted in *Numen* IV (1959): 77–95.

7. See my "An Appreciation," *Religions in Antiquity: Essays in Memory of Erwin Ramsdell Goodenough,* Jacob Neusner, ed. (Leiden, 1968), pp. 8–9.

8. Goodenough gave his exposition of his method of interpretation of symbols in his "The Evaluation of Symbols Recurrent in Time, as Illustrated in Judaism," *Eranos-Jahrbuch* XX (1951): 285–319.

9. The ship is presumably derived from the ferry boat of Charon which carried the souls of the departed to the abode of the dead. Rabbinic Judaism reflects a wide use of wine: at circumcision, marriage, the ushering in of the Sabbath and at its departure. There is no biblical basis for this use of wine. What is its origin? Is it possibly adopted from the mysteries of Dionysus?

10. I had many conversations with Dr. Goodenough. One came after the publication of the first two volumes of his *Jewish Symbols*. He felt aggrieved at the attacks on him, but even more on misunderstandings of his intent. I thereupon made the statement that there was no exposition in the first two volumes of what it was he was about. We debated the matter. Apparently I persuaded him, for in volume IV, pp. 2–44, he wrote at length about his purposes. It would have been so much better had he done so in volume I.

11. See Morton Smith, "Goodenough's *Jewish Symbols,*" *Journal of Biblical Literature* LXXXVI (1967): 53–68, and my *The First Christian Century in Judaism and Christianity* (New York, 1969), pp. 125–27 and p. 141, note 14. Smith, in providing a critique of Goodenough, declares the basic effort a failure: "Columbus failed, too. But his failure revealed a new world, and so did Goodenough's. . . . The extent and importance of the Jewish iconic material was practically unrealized before Goodenough's collection of it."

## Chapter 12

1. The following passage is from my *The First Christian Century in Judaism and Christianity* (New York, 1969), p. 137: "When any two civilizations encounter each other, as in the encounter by the Jewish civilization of the Greek civilization, they . . . fashion an intermediary civilization . . . always fraught with some sense of seeming alien to those in the respective civilizations who have not been part of the encounter. It is in such terms that a Paul and a

Philo seem so un-Jewish to so many Jewish commentators, and so un-Greek to so many classical commentators."

2. Key passages in this latter development are Eccles. 4:24; 9:1 and Wisdom of Solomon 4:11–19.

3. There has at times been an undue and untenable set of exaggerations about "wisdom"; see R. H. Whybray, *The Intellectual Tradition in the Old Testament* (Berlin, 1974). That exaggerations and resultant distortions of the dimensions of "wisdom" seem to have occurred does not nullify the residual importance of the motif.

4. Henry Chadwick, "St. Paul and Philo," *Bulletin of the John Rylands Library* XLVIII (1965–66): 286 ff.; Wilfred L. Knox, *St. Paul and the Church of Jerusalem* (Cambridge, 1925), has a list of passages (pp. 129–36) in which Paul and Philo echo each other. Knox (p. 135) goes on to say that "it is by no means unreasonable to suppose that the resemblances between the thought of S. Paul and Philo are attributable to their common use of other writings now lost, which put forward the allegorical interpretation of Judaism on lines somewhat less radical than those favoured by Philo, and more in accordance with the letter of the O.T. and its traditional rabbinical interpretation. It is however quite possible that S. Paul may well have had some slight general acquaintance with Philo. . . . At the same time the probability is very strongly in favour of the view that . . . both S. Paul and Philo are acquainted with and make use of the general outlook of Hellenistic Jewish thought. . . ."

5. Gerald Friedlander, *Hellenism and Christianity* (London, 1930), pp. 84 ff.

6. The Epistle to the Ephesians is almost universally denied to Paul, while it is debated whether Colossians is authentically by him.

7. The case seems right that in Paul the dualism between spirit and body is modified by his use of soul as a third entity, with soul at times apparently conceived of as related to body, but at other times to spirit.

8. It is an appendix, pp. 370–413, in Goodenough *BLL*.

9. On the details, and the allegation of inconsistencies, see Goodenough, "Law in the Subjective Realm," cited in note 8, especially pp. 372–86.

10. *Ibid.*, p. 394.

11. It is found in *Religions in Antiquity*, Jacob Neusner, ed. (Leiden, 1968), pp. 23–68.

12. Goodenough endorses the view of George Foot Moore, *Judaism*, I, pp. 479–96, and the even older view of Frank C. Porter, "The Yeçer Hara: A Study in the Jewish Doctrine of Sin," *Biblical and Semitic Studies* (New Haven, 1902), pp. 93–156, that the Rabbinic conceptions of the evil and good impulses are "quite different from the hellenistic idea widely held in the time of Paul, i.e., that these two impulses were centered, one in a superior part of man like the soul, and the other in the body" (pp. 56–57). Goodenough goes on (p. 57): "I can state positively that the doctrine that sin is a product of the body, that the law of sin is a part of the body, is quite hellenistic."

13. London, 1958. But see E. P. Sanders, *Paul and Palestinian Judaism* (Philadelphia, 1977). Sanders seems to shatter the thesis of Davies, this in concluding that Paul cannot be explained by resource to Palestinian Jewish documents. In a review of Sanders (*Religious Studies Review* (1978), I commented that Sanders does not proceed from his negative case into any rounded alternative, as for example, Paul as a Hellenistic person.

14. See my forthcoming "Apocalypse and Philo," *Jewish Quarterly Review*.

15. An essay by A. W. Argyle, "Philo and the Fourth Gospel," in *Expository Times* (LXIII 1951): pp. 385–86, affirms a direct Philonic influence on John. Robert McLachlen Wilson, "Philo and the Fourth Gospel," *ibid.*, LXV (1953): 47–49, contends that both drew on a relatively common environment.

16. I have not been persuaded that the prologue is a pre-Christian gnostic hymn. In *Judaism and Christian Beginnings* (New York, 1978), pp. 373–74, I gave an interpretation along this line, that Jews and Christians in common sought for communion with the Logos. The prologue is a Christian argument addressed to Jews, asserting that the quest for the Logas is no longer necessary, for the Logos and Jesus were one and the same.

17. In "Recent Discoveries in Palestine and the Gospel of St. John," *The Background of the New Testament and its Eschatology*, W. D. Davies and David Daube, eds. (Cambridge, 1956), pp. 153–71.

18. *Judentum und Hellenismus*[2] (Tübingen, 1973). See p. 157. L. H. Feldman, "Hengel's *Judaism and Hellenism*, in Retrospect," *Journal of Biblical Literature* XCVI (1977), is a long and thorough-going critique, or even refutation, of Hengel's viewpoint.

19. "Mark as a Redactor and Theologian: A Survey of Some Recent
    Markan Studies," *Journal of Biblical Literature* XC (1971), III:
    333–36. I have replied to this view in "Palestinian and Hellenistic
    Judaism and Christianity: The Question of the Comfortable
    Theory," scheduled to appear in a *Hebrew Union College Annual*
    L (1979).

20. Louis H. Feldman, *Studies in Judaica: Scholarship on Philo and
    Josephus, 1937–62* (New York, 1962), p. 20, cites S. Lyonnet,
    "L'Hymne christolgique de l'Epitre aux Colossiens et la fête juive
    du nouve An," *Recherches de Science Religieuse* LVIII (1960):
    93–100 (which I have not seen). Feldman reports that the author
    feels that the passage echoes *Spec*. II, 192. I have not seen a close
    connection.

21. I have not seen L. M. Cogdon's 1968 Ph.D. thesis, "The False
    Teachers at Colossae: Affinities with Essene and Philonic
    Thought"; a summary appears in *Dissertation Abstracts* XXIX
    (1968): 1591 A.

22. See G. W. H. Lampe and K. J. Woolcombe, *Essays on Typology*
    Naperville, 1957), especially pp. 64 ff. I am not sure that the dis-
    tinctions presented between allegorism and typology are always
    valid, for the reason that typology seems to be viewed as quite
    legitimate and allegory not.

23. In "Le philonisme de l'Epître aux Hébreux," *Revue Biblique* LVI
    (1949): 542–72, and LVII (1950): 212–42.

24. R. Williamson, *Philo and the Epistle to the Hebrews* (Leiden,
    1970), not only rejects Spicq's view, but also is skeptical of any
    direct relationship. Williamson is especially critical of theories of
    relationship based solely on linguistic studies; rather, one needs to
    look at themes and topics. Influences such as Scripture are deemed
    infinitely greater than the exaggeration of direct Philonic influ-
    ence. I have not seen a refutation of Spicq by F. Schröger, *Der
    Verfasser des Hebräerbrief als Schriftausleger* (Regensburg, 1968).
    *The Anchor Bible to the Hebrews*, 1972, by a former student,
    George Buchanan, seems to me without adequate balance. Bu-
    chanan interprets, indeed misinterprets, Hebrews as if it is a
    midrashic work of Rabbinic provenience. He believes it was writ-
    ten in Jerusalem between the death of Jesus and prior to A.D. 70.
    Philo does not appear in the Index, though some Philonic treatises
    appear in the bibliography.

25. This is mentioned in Irenaeus, *Adv. Haer.* I, 28, and Clement of Alexandria, *Stromata* VII, 17, and elsewhere.

26. See 1 John 4:1–3 and 2 John 7. Some see docetism in Col. 2:8, but this is disputed.

27. *Abr.* 107–18.

28. I have not seen F. R. M. Hitchcock, "Philo and the Pastorals," *Hermathena* LVI (1940): 113-35, nor H. G. Meechan, "The Epistle of St. James," *Expository Times* XLIX (1937–38): 181–83, which suggests that a disciple of Philo edited this epistle. Both are cited in Feldman, *op. cit.*, pp. 19–20. Both find similarities in the vocabulary of these Christian writers and Philo.

29. A word of explanation may be useful. When Philo makes Abraham's journey from Ur to Charran a spiritual journey that we too can make, he is de-historicizing the biblical narrative. He re-historicizes in that he makes the Abraham of history the man who long ago made a spiritual journey, and who reached perfection through instruction.

30. In *Jüdisch-christicher Schulbetrieb in Alexandrie und Rom. Literarische Untersuchungen zu Philo und Clemens von Alexandria, Justin und Irenäus* (Göttingen, 1915).

31. In "Philo and the Beginnings of Christian Thought," *The Cambridge History of Later Greek and Early Medieval Philosophy*, A. H. Armstrong, ed. (Cambridge, 1967), pp. 137–92. Chadwick quotes the high assessment of Philo by Eusebius, Jerome, and Augustine.

32. *Ecclesiastical History* II, 17:1. Professor Chadwick (*ibid.*, p. 157, note 4) cites another legend of Philo's being introduced to St. John. On these legends, see J. Edgar Bruns, "Philo Christianus: The Debris of a Legend," *Harvard Theological Review* 66 (1973): 141–45.

# A Select Bibliography

Arnold, W. T. *The Roman System of Provincial Administration*. Oxford: B. H. Blackwell, 1914.

Baer, Richard A., Jr. *Philo's Use of the Categories Male and Female*. Leiden: E. J. Brill, 1970.

Balsdon, J. P. V. D. *The Emperor Gaius*.[2] Oxford: Clarendon Press, 1964.

Bamberger, B. J. "The Dating of Aggadic Materials." *Journal of Biblical Literature* LXVIII (1949): 115-23.

Belkin, Samuel. *Philo and the Oral Law*. Cambridge, Mass.: Harvard University Press, 1940.

Bell, H. I. "Antisemitism at Alexandria." *Journal of Roman Studies* XXXI (1941): 1-18.

————. *Jews and Christians in Egypt*. Oxford: Oxford University Press, 1924.

Cohn, Leopold, "Einteilung und Chronologie der Schriften Philos," *Philologus*, Supp. VII (1899): 387-435.

*Corpus Papyrorum Judaicarum*. Edited by Victor A. Tcherikover and Alexander Fuks. 3 vols. Cambridge, Mass.: Published for Magnes Press, Hebrew University, by Harvard University Press, 1957-1964.

Drummond, James. *Philo Judaeus*. 2 vols. London: Williams and Norgate, 1888; reprinted, Amsterdam, 1969.

Fraser, P. M. "Foundation date of the Alexandrian Politeuma." *Harvard Theological Review* LIV (1961): 141-45.

Goodenough, Erwin R. *By Light, Light*. London: H. Milford, Oxford University Press, 1935.

———. *An Introduction to Philo Judaeus*. 2nd. ed. Oxford: Basil Blackwell, 1962.

———. *Jurisprudence of the Jewish Courts in Egypt*. New Haven: Yale University Press, 1929.

———. "Philo's Exposition of the Law and his *De Vita Mosis*." *Harvard Theological Review* XXVI (1933): 109–25.

———. *The Politics of Philo Judaeus*. New Haven: Yale University Press, 1938.

Hadas, Moses. *Hellenistic Culture*. New York: Columbia University Press, 1959.

Hagner, Donald A. "The Vision of God in Philo and John; A Comparative Study." *Journal of the Evangelical Theological Society* XIV (1971): 81–93.

Heinemann, Isaak. *Philons Griechische und Judische Bildung*. Hildesheim: Georg Olms Verlags-buchhandlung, 1962.

Jones, A. H. M. *The Cities of the Eastern Roman Provinces*. Oxford: Clarendon Press, 1937.

———. *The Greek City*. Oxford: Clarendon Press, 1940.

Jones, H. Stuart. "Claudius and the Jewish Question at Alexandria." *Journal of Roman Studies* XVI (1926): 17–35.

Katz, Peter. *Philo's Bible*. Cambridge, England: Cambridge University Press, 1950.

Leisegang, Hans. "Philo Judaeus von Alexandria." *Die Religion in Geschichte und Gegenwart*, 1930. Vol. V.

———. "Philon von Alexandria." *Paulys Real-Encyclopaedie*. 1950. Vol. XX.

Marcus, Ralph. "Jewish and Greek Elements in the LXX." *Louis Ginzberg Jubilee Volume*. New York: n.p., 1945.

———. "Recent Literature on Philo (1924–1934)." *Jewish Studies in Memory of George A[lexander] Kohut*. New York: n.p., 1935.

Massebieau, M. L. *Le Classement des Oeuvres de Philon*. Paris: La Bibliotheque de l'Ecole des Hautes Études Section des Science religieuses, 1889.

Momigliano, Arnaldo. *Claudius*. Translated by W. D. Hogarth. Oxford: Clarendon Press, 1934.

Nikiprowetzsky, Valentin. *Le Commentaire de l'Ecriture chez Philon d'Alexandrie*, Lille, 1974.

Nock, A. D. "Notes on Ruler-Cult." *Journal of Hellenic Studies* XLVIII (1928): 21–43.

———. "Religious Development from the Close of the Republic to the Death of Nero." *Cambridge Ancient History*. Vol. X. New York: Macmillan Co., 1934.

Rostovtzeff, Michael I. *Social and Economic History of the Hellenistic World*. 3 vols. Oxford: Clarendon Press, 1941.

———. *Social and Economic History of the Roman Empire*. Oxford: Clarendon Press, 1926.

Sandmel, Samuel. *Philo's Place in Judaism*.[2] New York: Ktav Publishing House, Inc. 1971.

Shroyer, Montgomery J. "Alexandrian Jewish Literalists." *Journal of Biblical Literature* LV (1936): 261–84.

Simon, M. "Situation du judaïsme alexandrin dans la diaspora." *Philon d'Alexandrie*. Lyons, 1966. Colloques Nationaux du Centre de la Recherche Scientifique, VII. Paris, 1967.

Smallwood, E. Mary. "Jews and Romans in the Early Empire." *History Today* XV (1965): 232–39, 313–19.

———. *Philonis Alexandrini, Legatio ad Gaium*. Leiden: E. J. Brill, 1961.

———. *The Jews under Roman Rule. From Pompey to Diocletian*. Leiden, 1976.

Stein, Edmund. *Die allegorische Exegese des Philo aus Alexandreia*. Giessen: A. Toepelmann, 1929.

———. *Philo und der Midrasch*. Giessen: A. Toepelmann, 1931.

Tcherikover, Victor. *Hellenistic Civilization and the Jews*. Tr. by S. Applebaum. Philadelphia: Jewish Publication Society of America, 1959.

Williamson, Ronald. *Philo and the Epistle to the Hebrews*. Arbeiten zur Literatur und Geschichte Des Hellenistischen Judentums. Vol. IV. Leiden: E. J. Brill, 1970.

Wolfson, Harry A. *Philo*. 2 vols. Cambridge, Mass.: Harvard University Press, 1947.

Zielinski, Thadee. "L'empereur Claude et l'idee de la domination mondiale des Juifs." *Revue de l'Université de Bruxelles* XXXII (1926–1927): 113–48.

# Index

Genesis, 56–57
Gentiles and Jewish writings, 47
*Gerousia*, 41, 106
Ginzberg, Louis, 133
Glatzer, N., 181
Gnostic, gnosticism, 135–39
God, 50–51, 59–62, 67, 73, 89–92, 114;
    as Ruler, 61; as Creator, 53; and
    *Physis*, 122; Father of Isaac, 86;
    Nameless, 93
Goodenough, Erwin R., 11, 47, 78,
    138, 140–47, 152–54, 166, 178, 183,
    186, 189, 190, 191, 192
Goodhart, H. L., 166
Graces, 59, 85
"Great Mother," 143
Greek language, 51–52, 119
*Gymnasia*, 9, 12

Haase, W., 166
Hagar (encyclical studies), 19, 21,
    25, 85, 162
Haggada, halacha, 128–32
Harl, Marguerite, 124, 186
Harnack, Adolf von, 136
Hasidism, 134
Heaven, 116
Hebrew (language), 27–28, 131
Hebrews, Epistle to the, 4, 160–61
Heinemann, Isaac, 133
Hell, 116
Hellenization, 118, 122, 134, 141–44,
    147
Hengel, Martin, 157, 188
Hercules, 180
Herod the Great, 3, 11, 103
*Hieros logos*, 95
High Priest, 95
Higher mind, 25, 62, 99, 100, 116,
    153–54
Hilgert, Earle, 166, 167
Hillel, 3, 21–22, 129
History, 25, 162; dissolution of,
    149–50
History of Religions, 140–43
Hitchcock, F. R. M., 194
Hokma, 98–99, 148

Homer, 19, 38
Hope, 58, 84
Howard, George, 177
*Humanity, On*, 69
Hyatt, J. P., 188
Hypostasis, 149
*Hypothetica*, 31

Ideas, 95, 97; *see also* Powers
Immortality, 51, 100, 117
Incarnate Law, see *Nomos
    empsychos*
Incarnation, 155
Instruction, 58, 61; *see also* Abraham
Intelligible world, 25, 54–55, 60, 92,
    95, 97, 150
Intuition, *see* Isaac
Irenaeus, 193
Isaac (intuition; joy), 25–26, 56, 58,
    62, 85–86, 104, 114
*Isopoliteia*, 8–9
Israel (seer of God), 59, 73, 87–88

Jacob (practice), 25–26, 58, 85–87,
    104
Jamnia, 127
Jesus, 3, 135, 141
Jewett, R., 189
Jews, 101, 103, 119; see also
    *Politeuma*
John, Gospel According to, 136–37,
    154, 157
Jonas, Hans, 137
Jones, H. S., 172
Joseph, 56, 63–65, 103
*Joseph, On*, 49, 63–65
Josephus, 7–9, 23–24, 39, 130, 141,
    173, 175, 186
Joshua, 70, 104–5
Joy, 114; *see also* Isaac
Jubilees, 56, 130, 176, 186
Judaism, 109, 113, 174
Judaization, 122
Judea, 102, 107, 110
Julius Caesar, 8
Jung, Carl, 145